★ ★ ★ ★ ★ ★ ★ ★ ★

Women
IN THE
Military

★ ★ ★ ★ ★ ★ ★ ★ ★

★ Sandra Carson Stanley ★

Julian Ⓜ Messner

To All Who Serve

With Special Thoughts of Those
Who Made The Greatest Sacrifice
By Giving Their Lives In Service

And

To The Young People of America

May You Learn The Value of Service
And Accept The Opportunities and
Challenges It Offers

Design by Paula R. Szafranski

Manufactured in the United States of America

10   9   8   7   6   5   4   3   2   1 (LSB)
10   9   8   7   6   5   4   3   2   1 (pbk)

Library of Congress Cataloging-in-Publication Data
Stanley, Sandra Carson.
    Women in the military / by Sandra Carson Stanley.
        p.   cm.
    Includes bibliographical references and index.
    Summary: A variety of women in the military services discuss such
issues as enlistment, job opportunities, promotion
potential, sexual harassment, family life, working with male
colleagues, and combat roles for women.
    1. United States—Armed Forces—Women—Juvenile literature.
[1. United States—Armed Forces—Women.]   I. Title.
UB418.W65S73   1993
355'.0082—dc20   93-22312
                                                            CIP
ISBN 0-671-75549-8 (LSB)   AC
ISBN 0-671-75550-1 (pbk.)

Contents

Introduction   1

Chapter 1   Breaking Ground: Women's Early Involvement in
Military Activities   9

Chapter 2   Gaining Ground: The Expansion Years—1970s and
1980s   27

Chapter 3   Women's Current Service in the Military   34

Chapter 4   Choices for Service: Branches, Active Duty,
Reserves, and National Guard   54

Chapter 5   Options for Service: Enlisted and Officer Ranks   65

Chapter 6   Becoming an Officer: How You Get There   85

Chapter 7   Looking Ahead: Future Prospects for Women in
the United States Military   107

Epilogue   113

Time Line   117
Glossary   119
Notes   123
Further Reading   129
Addresses for the United States Military Academies   130
Tables   131
Index   137

Acknowledgments

This work reflects the contributions of many people. The editorial assistance of Adriane Ruggiero was invaluable. Barbara Bradford and Colleen Arntz assisted in the preparation of the manuscript.

Experience is a meaningful teacher and I am most indebted to those who shared their time and personal experiences with me in conversations and interviews. Other military personnel and civilians provided information and insights which contributed to my understanding and the content of this book.

Many colleagues and friends have shared my interests and provided guidance and encouragement: William Boltz (University of Chicago), Charles Moskos (Northwestern University), Mady Wechsler Segal and David R. Segal (University of Maryland—College Park). I would also like to recognize members of the faculty and staff at Towson State University who have supported my efforts for many years: Irwin Goldberg, Justine Jones, R. Guy Sedlack, Jay Stanley, and Ida Ward. Dean Esslinger, Associate Dean of Faculty Development and Research, and his committees have supported my research with the valuable gift of time.

My network extends beyond the boundaries of the United States. I am grateful to Cheryl Lamerson and Judi Pinch, who currently serve, and to Rosemary Park and Franklin C. Pinch who recently retired from the Canadian Forces. I would also like to acknowledge

Reuven Gal and Ruth Linn who served in the Israeli Defense Forces and who helped me understand and appreciate differences.

I will always remember Morris Rosenberg and Nora Kinzer Stewart, whose untimely deaths leave a void in my life, but who continue to serve as mentors and influence my thoughts.

The friendship and interest offered by Joan and Richard Bader have been invaluable over the years. I am always mindful of the love and constant support offered by my parents, Loyd and Rosemary Carson, my sisters Marcia, Becky, and Paula, and their families.

Finally, I would like to recognize my husband, Jay, and our son, Hart. Jay's contributions, tangible and intangible, to this work and to my intellectual and personal life are countless. Hart has lived with a hassled and impatient mom and continues to be a source of perspective and joy. Thank you both for sharing my life.

Photo Acknowledgments

Page 3: Reuters/Bettmann. **Pages 10 and 12:** Culver Pictures. **Pages 13 and 15:** The Bettmann Archive. **Pages 16, 17, 19, 20:** UPI/Bettmann. **Page 29:** Bob Daemmrich/Stock•Boston. **Page 35:** United States Air Force. **Page 41:** N.R. Rowan/Stock•Boston. **Page 43:** United States Navy. **Page 45:** Used by permission of Marie Elliott. **Page 50:** United States Air Force. **Page 59:** Used by permission of Deborah Strevig. **Page 67:** N.R. Rowan/Stock•Boston. **Page 74:** United States Navy. **Page 78:** Used by permission of Kathryn Lindsay Townsend. **Pages 88 and 90:** United States Navy. **Page 92.** Used by permission of Andrea Louise Lemon. **Page 98:** UPI/Bettmann. **Page 101:** Used by permission of Katherine Elizabeth Simonson.

About the Author

Sandra Carson Stanley received a B.A. degree in sociology and psychology from Towson State University, a M.A. degree in clinical psychology from Loyola College, and a Ph.D. in sociology from the University of Maryland. She is an associate professor of sociology at Towson State University, a member of the Advisory Council of the Inter-University Seminar on Armed Forces and Society, and an associate editor for an international journal, *Armed Forces and Society*.

Dr. Stanley has published articles on women in armed forces and has given presentations on the subject in Canada, Israel, Switzerland, and the United States.

★ ★ ★ ★ ★ ★ ★ ★ ★ ★ ★ ★ ★ ★ ★ ★ ★ ★

Introduction

The mission of the United States armed forces, or military, is to protect and defend the nation and its interests. This is a huge task and requires complicated organization and the efforts of many people.

The **Department of Defense (DoD)**, an agency of the federal government, supervises the activities of the United States military. Four branches, or **services**—the Air Force, Army, Navy, and Marines— are under the authority of the DoD. The Coast Guard is under the direction of the Department of Transportation during peacetime, but is responsible to the DoD during times of national emergency, as during the 1990–1991 war in the Persian Gulf.

The military is the largest employer in the United States. As such, it offers many career choices and job opportunities. People who join the military may serve on a full-time basis, known as **active duty,** or on a part-time basis, in one of the **reserve** units. Specific information about these choices is included in Chapter 4.

As of January 30, 1992, there were 3,140,200 people serving in the military: 2,002,600 on active duty and 1,137,600 in the reserves. In addition, there were 1,044,500 civilians working for the armed forces and defense agencies.[1] Other civilians are employed by private companies that have contracts with the DoD for making weapons and equipment and providing other needed services.

Women have long contributed to our nation's defense. Today they serve in a variety of jobs in all branches of the service. As of September 1992, there were 357,183 women in the armed forces: 208,398 were on active duty and 148,785 were in the reserves. They made up 11.4 percent of the active duty forces and 13.3 percent of the reserves.[2] This level of participation has not always prevailed, however.

The Military—A Reflection of Society

A nation's military is in many ways a reflection of the society it protects and defends. Consequently, the United States armed forces like the armed forces of other nations, have been led and peopled by men. Women in the United States military continue to be a minority. Their inclusion has often been resisted by men and their contributions have been minimized or underappreciated.

Women are not the first group to face obstacles to their military participation. While African-American men took part in all conflicts in which the United States was involved, racial integration in the United States military did not take place until the early 1950s, during the conflict in Korea. Before Korea, African-American soldiers did not have the same opportunities as white soldiers.

In some ways the integration of women into the United States military has been similar to the integration of African-American men. Women have confronted barriers similar to those that kept blacks from full participation. Both groups have at times been officially excluded from the military, then allowed to serve during national emergencies when there were personnel shortages. When the crises ended, both groups were required to leave the service. In addition, quotas were used to limit the percentages of blacks and women who were allowed to enlist.

African-American men who did join the military served in segregated units, apart from white men. Both blacks and women were assigned certain jobs and could not serve in combat specialties, senior officer ranks, or command positions. Both were the target of negative attitudes and discrimination. Both felt they had to prove themselves worthy of the opportunities offered by a mainly white, mainly male military.

In spite of these discriminatory practices, African-Americans and women have found the military attractive because of job opportuni-

Women in the United States military are from all backgrounds and have a variety of reasons for being there. These soldiers, members of the 24th Infantry, took part in the Persian Gulf War.

ties and benefits such as health care, education, and skill training. This is especially true during times of economic hardship when jobs in civilian society are scarce. Even though members of minority groups have experienced limitations of opportunity, many believe the military to be less discriminatory than the civilian world. Their belief is due in part to the fact that pay and benefits are attached to rank, and promotion is based on meeting clearly specified requirements rather than on personal characteristics such as race or sex.[3]

Outsiders in a Male Environment?

While some women's experiences have been similar to those of black men, their integration into the military has also *differed* in several ways. Because of our society's fundamental belief that protecting the home and going to war are a man's work, men from minority groups have often been accepted more readily in the military than have women. Women have been viewed as outsiders in a male environment.

Other concerns about the inclusion of women have been raised—concerns not associated with black men's participation. One long-standing issue among military personnel and others is that women's *presumed* physical and psychological characteristics may interfere with their performance of some military jobs. For example, one consideration focuses on physical strength. Some fear that women may not be strong enough to lift and carry heavy equipment or wounded fellow soldiers and that they may lack the endurance to perform these tasks over a long period of time. There is also the fear that women may not have the physical strength to perform certain tasks quickly, such as loading heavy shells into a weapon. Those opposed to allowing women in combat units suggest that warfare does not allow for the weak or slow. Furthermore, these same opponents are quick to point out that such members might be responsible for getting other soldiers injured or killed.

Opponents of women in the military also argue that certain female biological characteristics may limit military effectiveness. It has been frequently assumed by the military and others that a woman's monthly menstrual cycle and/or her pregnancy might interfere with job performance and assignment overseas or to remote areas. Opponents also maintain that allowing women into an all-male environment may lead to increased costs in such areas as equipment and uniform modification (since women are typically smaller than men) and to altering sleeping areas and bathrooms (to provide privacy for male and female soldiers). These costly changes, the opponents argue, may reduce funds available for other items, such as more sophisticated weapons systems, that would more directly maintain or increase military effectiveness.

Ideas about women's psychological characteristics have also served as a basis for objections to their taking part in military activities. Throughout history, people in all societies have held **stereotypes** of the "ideal woman." These ideas are based on assumptions about psychological traits that a society believes are, or should be, characteristic of women. Some of these traits include warmth, a nurturing personality, submissiveness, lack of aggressiveness, and an emotional nature. Some people have suggested that these traits are incompatible with those traits believed to be essential for effective performance of military and combat jobs: aggression, emotional toughness, and stability.

Military officials have also considered whether the relationships within a military unit may be affected by the presence of women. A common notion is that women's presence will disrupt men's relationships with each other and thus interfere with the efficient functioning of the unit. Such a disruption *might* occur if the men compete with each other for the women's attention, or if the men feel the need to protect female soldiers from danger.[4] A *New York Times* article of July 21, 1991, reported that opponents of women's participation in combat believe women will destroy the "bonding" between men in a unit. The fighting efficiency of the unit will be further weakened, opponents believe, because men will expect less from female soldiers and take extra measures to care for them rather than perform their own duties. Some people believe that images of protecting women at home motivate men to fight and that the presence of women fighting beside men may reduce this motivation.

Other Issues

Potential problems arise any time a new group is introduced into an environment that has been dominated by another group. The issues and concerns associated with women's participation in the military are similar to those related to women's entry into other male-dominated environments, such as police work, fire-fighting, high-level management in the business world and, in earlier years, medicine and law.

Sexual discrimination and **sexual harassment** are major concerns of women in the male-dominated military world. Sexual discrimination involves unequal treatment of a person on the basis of their sex, rather than on the basis of their qualifications. Since the Department of Defense has expressed a commitment to providing women equal opportunity, discrimination is of lesser concern than harassment. Sexual harassment occurs when a person makes uninvited and unwelcome comments or advances of a sexual nature to another person. The harassment can range from making sexually suggestive comments to the use of pressure by a supervisor to obtain sexual favors to such serious crimes as rape or sexual assault. All types of sexual harassment are demeaning and embarrassing to the victim. The number of sexual harassment cases reported by women in the military has increased dramatically in the past few years. Perhaps the most famous example is the Tailhook incident of 1991. At that time, a group of at least 140 naval officers attending a convention in Las Vegas, Nevada, verbally and physically harassed naval and civilian women in their hotel. The armed services have clear policies forbidding this kind of behavior and offenders are punished. The scandal was a major embarrassment for the Navy and resulted in the resignation of the secretary of the Navy in June of 1992.[5]

Military women are by no means the only victims of sexual harassment. Women in all types of jobs may experience the problem. It does seem that it is more likely to happen to women in traditionally male jobs. It is also possible, but less likely, for men to be harassed in this way.

In addition to sexual harassment, military women and those in other male-dominated worlds often experience other negative attitudes. They can meet resistance to their presence, which then leads to lack of acceptance. Men's attitudes and behaviors, whether expressed openly or indirectly, may create stress for women. Many military women have reported feeling pressure to perform or to "prove" themselves in their job assignments.[6]

Fraternization, the development of close personal relationships, has always been an issue in the military. In years past, the military was concerned about the possible formation of friendships between superiors and subordinates, or between officers and enlisted personnel. The presence of women in the military has added a new dimension to the issue. Now there exists the possibility of close personal relationships between men and women as well as between officers and enlisted personnel. The military realizes that fraternization may cause problems by interfering with morale, discipline, and the successful completion of a mission. In response, each of the armed services has established regulations that define acceptable relationships between officers and enlisted personnel and between men and women.

Open admission of homosexuality is now just gaining attention as an issue. At present, such an admission prevents people from joining the military, and discovery of this preference is grounds for discharge. Lesbianism is viewed as a possible problem related to womens' presence in the military. While the military strictly forbids homosexuality for both men and women, some women believe they are more likely to be accused and investigated than are men.[7] Congress and the United States military will continue to debate and discuss the issue of gays and lesbians in the armed services.

It is important to note that the concerns just described are related to opinions about women's *presumed* traits and capabilities and *assumptions* about the impact of their presence on military effectiveness and interpersonal relationships. Not all women possess the so-called feminine traits. Some men have them too. When any group is defined by stereotypes, the people within that group are treated as a category—in this case, women—and not as individuals. Many opinions about women in the military are based on *assumptions*, rather that *facts*. But systematic evaluations of women's military performance by the Department of Defense and the separate armed services have not supported the assumptions about their negative impact.[8]

Some of the more recent considerations associated with women's military participation concern equal opportunity and "quality of life" issues. Discrimination in the recruitment of women, the assignment of jobs, and career development once they are in the military fall under the equal opportunity category. "Quality of life" issues include adequacy of services (such as medical care) and recreational facilities. For example, military women have complained about the types of entertainment available on bases. Many feel they are in poor taste and degrade women.

Family needs are also included in the "quality of life" category. Reliable and affordable child care is a concern for many military families, especially for single parents and joint service couples (those in which both husband and wife are in the military). These military men and women face difficulties when their work hours are irregular or when they are sent away from their home base for military operations. Another major concern for joint service couples is that they be assigned to locations that are close together.[9]

Women in the United States military face many challenges, as individuals and as a group, as we move into the twenty-first century. Some of the challenges are long-standing and others are new. While

7

the situation for military women has improved over the years, they continue to work for greater acceptance and equality. Assignment to new positions, especially those involving combat, and a greater number of promotions to the senior officer ranks represent two goals of military women. These goals and the long-standing challenges facing these women take on new meaning in light of the plans to reduce the size of the American armed forces. Whatever the challenges, women will probably continue to gain ground in the military in the next century. Their future is filled with many interesting and exciting possibilities.

This book tells the stories of several women who are currently serving in the United States military and one who recently retired from service. They describe their reasons for joining, their involvement, the benefits and problems associated with their service, and the nature and meaning of service to their country. Through them you will learn about the challenges that military women have faced and continue to face in the 1990s.

★ ★ ★ ★ ★ ★ ★ ★ ★ ★ ★ ★ ★ ★ ★ ★ ★ ★ ★

CHAPTER
ONE

Breaking Ground:
Women's Early Involvement
in Military Activities

Women have been involved in all wars in which the United States has been engaged. In the early years they took part in a variety of military activities, but almost always in unofficial and unconventional ways because they were not allowed to serve in conventional ways. In fact, this has been true in many nations throughout history.

"Molly Pitcher"

During the American Revolution, civilian women often followed their husbands' fighting units and frequently took their children with them. Historians have called these women and their children "campfollowers." The women performed various tasks in support of the troops. They nursed the sick and wounded, cooked meals, washed laundry, and helped to set up and break camp. They also helped soldiers on the battlefield by carrying pitchers of water to cool the cannons after firing. The nickname "Molly Pitcher" originated in reference to these women. Sometimes the women picked up the weapons of injured men and joined the fighting.

Other women were more directly involved in military activities. These activities included espionage, defense of local communities, and enlistment in regular fighting units. The women who did join the troops disguised themselves as men and enlisted under men's names.[1]

No one knows for sure the true identity of "Molly Pitcher," the heroine of the Battle of Monmouth. Some historians say she was Mary Hays, wife of an artilleryman whose gun position was severely hit during battle. Mary took up a staff and helped load the cannon until replacements arrived.

Deborah Samson, who enlisted as Robert Shurtliff, is probably the most famous of the male impersonators. She was self-educated and became a schoolteacher before joining a Massachusetts regiment in May 1782. Samson was respected by her fellow soldiers but was forced to leave her unit in October 1783, when a physician who was treating her for illness discovered that she was a woman. Her efforts to serve as a soldier were recognized many years later. In 1983 Deborah Samson was named the Official Heroine of the Commonwealth of Massachusetts and, in 1985, was honored with the Commemorative Medal by the United States Capitol Society.

Interestingly, much of the published information about Deborah Samson appears to have been based on fiction rather than fact. One of the most frequent errors has been found in the misspelling of her last name. It has often been written as Sampson rather than Samson, the correct spelling. While she has frequently been referred to as "America's First Woman Warrior," there is some evidence that several other women dressed as men and joined fighting units a few years earlier.[2]

During the Civil War and After

In the nineteenth century the role of women in United States military efforts saw little change from this early pattern. Women continued to be used whenever and however they were needed. Often they were not paid, and if they were paid for their services they were seen as serving *with* and not *in* the armed forces. In other words, they were not considered to be an official part of the military.

Women performed various duties during the Civil War. Civilian women from the Union and Confederate sides performed necessary support functions such as cooking, washing laundry, and nursing the sick and wounded. All of these were arduous tasks, considering the difficult circumstances. Clothing was boiled in heavy tubs, cooking was done out-of-doors most of the time, and bodies had to be lifted and moved. Women had to be strong, and they were.

Women also assisted the opposing armies in unconventional ways. Some served as couriers and carried war funds and documents hidden in their clothing. Others acted as spies, saboteurs, guides, scouts, and gun runners. The abolitionist Harriet Tubman helped Union forces in South Carolina as a cook, nurse, guide, and spy. Less well-known women also risked their lives. Mary Jane Green of West Virginia was arrested and sent to jail for spying for the Union army. Lila Greet of Alabama worked with a demolition team to burn a railroad bridge over the Tennessee River. This act of sabotage prevented supplies from getting to the Union army. Belle Boyd barely escaped capture several times and was finally arrested while she was employed as a courier by the Confederate government.

Women also disguised themselves as men and joined fighting units. Malinda Black joined a North Carolina unit with her husband. She posed as his younger brother and they fought together in three battles. She revealed her identity and resigned when her husband was discharged because of illness.

During the Civil War, thousands of volunteer nurses and other women provided medical supplies and nursing care on the battlefield. Others cared for the sick and wounded in hospitals such as this one in Washington, D.C.

Amy Clark enlisted as Richard Anderson in her husband's Louisiana cavalry unit. They served together for seven months before she left to join a unit in Tennessee. Husband and wife both fought in the battle at Shiloh. When Clark's husband was killed, she buried him and continued to fight. Later she was wounded and taken prisoner at a battle in Richmond. When her sex was discovered, she was freed and required to put on women's clothes before she was sent back to the South.

Some women were recognized for distinguished service and promoted to higher officer ranks. In most instances, however, they were discharged if their female identities were discovered.[3]

Women's contributions to medical care were the most widely recognized aspect of women's participation in the Civil War. Clara Barton and Dorothea Lynde Dix set up nursing services for the Union. Dr. Mary E. Walker served as the first female physician in the Army. However, these women always served as civilians. They were

Dr. Mary Walker, an early feminist, served with the Medical Corps during the Civil War. She became the first woman doctor in the Army and was awarded the Congressional Medal of Honor for outstanding service.

never granted military status, and despite the importance of their contributions, they were not seen as an essential or permanent part of the military. When the war ended in 1865, women, including nurses, were sent home.[4]

Women's desire to serve continued and the military continued to use them. During the Spanish-American War, female nurses were needed because there were not enough male medical personnel to care for American troops affected by a typhoid epidemic. Approximately fifteen hundred nurses were employed under contract to the military as civilian workers, rather than as uniformed members of the military. In recognition of their contributions, the government drafted legislation giving nurses quasi-military status.[5]

Women first wore uniforms and officially participated in the United States military when the Nursing Corps was established as an ·y unit by the Army (1901) and Navy (1908). The nurses ied important functions for the services but did not hold ry rank or receive the same pay or retirement and veterans' ·fits as male soldiers and veterans. Interestingly, the women who ed their country were not allowed to vote in United States elections, since American women were not granted the right to vote until 1920.

In World War I

When it appeared that the United States would enter World War I and personnel shortages in administrative jobs were anticipated, the military recruited women for jobs similar to those they held in civilian society. This meant clerical work and operating telephones. Approximately thirteen thousand women served as **yeomen (F)** in the Naval Reserve and Marine Corps Reserve (F). The term *yeoman* was used to refer to people who performed clerical jobs; the *F* in their title indicated that they were females. While most did perform these traditional female duties, some took over "men's jobs," such as drafting, recruiting, translating, and designing camouflage equipment. Women served in the United States and overseas. Several earned medals, and although women were not assigned to combat duties, they were exposed to risk. Approximately two hundred women were killed during World War I.[6]

The female reservists who served during the war were the first American women to be granted full military rank and status. This meant that they were subject to the same service obligation and disciplinary rules as men and received the same pay and allowances. However, their advancement was limited, since they could not be promoted above the rank of sergeant. When the war ended, most of the women were discharged and the American military was once again a male world. Female veterans of World War I were given the same benefits as male veterans.

During World War I, the Navy and Marine Corps authorized the recruit-ment of female yeoman (popularly known as "yeomanettes") to perform specific jobs and free men to fight.

Approximately thirty-six thousand women served in the Army and Navy Nurse Corps between 1917 and 1918, the period of America's involvement in the war. They were stationed in the United States and overseas in France, Belgium, England, Italy, Russia, Hawaii, Puerto Rico, and the Philippine Islands. They were assigned to hospitals in the field, on trains, and on ships, as well as to regular military bases. The nurses did not receive full military status, as did the women in the Naval and Marine Corps Reserves, and they were not discharged as quickly as the reservists when the war ended.

Civilian women, under contract, worked in clerical and adminis-trative jobs for the Army. No women were employed as military personnel by the Army during World War I.[7]

World War I saw women move into the workforce in great numbers. As industries stepped up production, women were hired in factories, steel mills, munitions plants, and, like the worker shown here, in shipyards.

In World War II

The pattern of using women in time of national need repeated itself when the United States military confronted personnel shortages after Japan's attack on Pearl Harbor in December 1941. With the United States in the war, the Army, Navy, Marines, and Coast Guard formed women's branches, separate from those of men. In 1942 the Army established the **Women's Auxiliary Army Corps (WAAC).** Its first director was publisher, lawyer, and writer Oveta Culp Hobby. A short time later the Navy formed the women's reserves known as **Women Accepted for Volunteer Emergency Service (WAVES).** Its first leader was the colorful Mildred McAfee. The Marine Corps and Coast Guard followed with the creation of women's reserve units.

The designations "auxiliary" (Army) and "reserve" (Navy, Marines, and Coast Guard) had important implications for the women who joined. Those who held auxiliary status in the Army (WAAC)

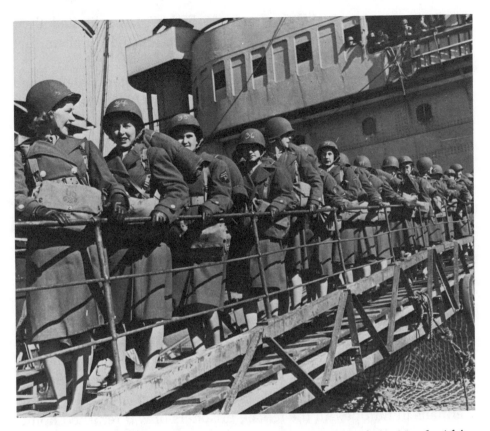

Members of the Women's Army Corps (WAC) disembark in North Africa during World War II. The integration of the WAC into the Army with full military status showed the public that the Army wanted and needed women.

did not receive the same pay, benefits, or rank as did the men who were regular members of the Army. For this reason, the Army had fewer female volunteers than did the other services. In response to the recruitment shortage, the Army changed the auxiliary status and the Women's Auxiliary Army Corps (WAAC) became known as the **Women's Army Corps (WAC)** in 1943. This change improved the status of Army women.

Although women who joined the reserve units in the Navy, Marines, and Coast Guard had more opportunities than women who served in auxiliary units in World War I, the conditions of their service were still not equal to those of men. Women were in separate branches from the men and did not receive combat training, since their purpose was to "Free a man to Fight." Laws limited their promotion to higher officer ranks and restricted the numbers that were allowed to enlist in the military.

Approximately 350,000 women served in the United States armed forces during World War II. Although most held "traditional" women's jobs in health care, administration, and clerical work, some performed duties usually reserved for men. These women worked as parachute riggers, mechanics, and weapons instructors. Certain jobs in aviation were open to women in World War II, but no military women served as pilots.[8] Some worked in air traffic control, while others served as instructors or as air crew members (operating various types of equipment on aircraft).

Although women were not assigned to combat jobs, many served overseas in combat zones. Like the men, they served under extremely harsh conditions. Reportedly, eighty-two military women were taken as prisoners of war. Forty-six of them are still alive. Some of them include Dorothy Arnold, Ruby Bradley, Hattie Brantley, Mary Rose Harrington Nelson, and Helen Cassini Nestor. While the majority were captured in the Pacific area, an army nurse, Second Lieutenant Reba Zitella Whittle, was shot down and held by the Germans in Europe. All the female prisoners of war returned home. Approximately two hundred nurses died in Europe and the Pacific during the war. More than sixteen hundred women received medals for their distinguished service.[9]

The United States did not join two of its major allies (the Soviet Union and Great Britain) in drafting women into the military during World War II. Although three formal proposals to draft women along with men were considered by the United States government, the legislation was not enacted. All women who served in the American military during World War II were volunteers.

Civilian women also supported the war effort. Approximately one thousand served as **Women Airforce Service Pilots (WASPs)**. Under the leadership of famed pilot Jacqueline Cochran, the WASPs flew under military rules and discipline, but held civil-service, not military, status. As we have said, military women were not allowed to fly military aircraft. The WASPs served as test pilots, as instructors, and trained men for flight duty. In addition, they flew all types of military aircraft, including fighters and bombers, to military bases

The WASPs flew planes from factories in the United States to bases overseas. The Army Air Force welcomed their contribution with enthusiasm.

overseas. However, they did not fly combat missions. Thirty-eight WASPs died while performing their duties. In 1977 the surviving members of the WASPs—including Grace Binge Mayfield, Dawn Rochow Seymour, and Barbara Jean Erikson London—were granted veteran status by the United States Congress. This entitled them to receive benefits from the **Veterans Administration (VA)**. Barbara Jean Erikson London, who flew thirty-six types of airplanes overseas, received the Air Medal in honor of her outstanding service.[10]

On the Home Front

Many women joined the civilian labor force for the first time during World War II. They worked in munitions factories, on assembly lines, and in other war-related industries. The nickname ''Rosie the Riveter'' has often been used to refer to these women who performed civilian jobs usually performed by men.

At the end of World War II most military women returned to civilian life. Those who remained in the service took on less

As men were called up to combat in increasing numbers, more and more women took over jobs in the civilian world. In 1943 there were approximately fourteen hundred women employed in this Washington, D.C., naval yard. Head coverings kept long hair from getting caught in machinery.

important positions. Still, World War II is considered the turning point in the history of women's military participation because of the significance of their contributions. Many civilian women who held jobs during the war also were sent home to make room for men who were being discharged by the military.

The pattern of sending women home after a crisis had ended was repeated. In past wars, women had been used whenever and however they were needed but were expected to return to more conventional "female" behavior when the situation became more normal. Following World War II, women's return to the home reflected the mood of the country. It was a time when people wanted the security of prewar values and roles. Given this environment, women had to take a step back in their ambitions.

An Important Act

Peacetime brought its own challenges to the military. And military women were part of the challenge. The **Women's Armed Services Integration Act** was passed in 1948. This act offered women regular military status but also imposed several restrictions on their service. Some of these restrictions remained in place for more than twenty years. For example, the act set limits for the percentages of enlisted women and female officers who could serve in the United States military. It also imposed restrictions on the recruitment of women, their career opportunities, and family benefits.

Perhaps the most important limitations on women's involvement were the **combat exclusions** for women in the Air Force, Navy, and Marines. The 1948 act prohibited these women from serving on combat aircraft and, other than temporary duty, on most naval vessels except hospital ships, transports, and similar vessels not expected to be involved in combat missions. There was a loophole, however. The legal exclusions did *not* apply to the Army and did *not* specifically prohibit women from ground combat. But the Army got around the loophole by formulating an exclusion policy based on the interpretation of the content of the law's specifications for women in the other services. Since 1948 it has been policy, *not* law, that has restricted the service of Army women. Although the definitions of combat and use of the law have varied from time to time and from one branch of service to another, these exclusions remained in effect for more than forty years. Some exclusions continue to operate today.[11]

The Cold War Era

The time after World War II was dominated by concern with Soviet-American relations. During this period, called the Cold War by historians, friction between the two world superpowers resulted in a bipolar world. An alliance system of the Soviet Union and Com-

21

munist-dominated eastern European nations represented the "East" and formed the Warsaw Pact. The "West" consisted of the United States and its western European allies. The **North Atlantic Treaty Organization (NATO)** emerged from this alliance. Both the Warsaw Pact nations and NATO maintained large military forces prepared to respond to the potential threat caused by the tensions. While it is difficult to say exactly when the Cold War ended, the time since the fall of the Berlin Wall and the breakup of the Soviet Union in the late 1980s and early 1990s is referred to as the "post Cold War" period.

Approximately forty-nine thousand women served in the United States military at the height of the Korean conflict. Only nurses actually served in Korea. More women would have been allowed to enlist, but the military's recruitment goals fell short in part because the country's involvement was unpopular with the American people.[12]

During this time the Department of Defense became interested in attracting more women volunteers to serve in the military. The **Defense Advisory Committee on Women in the Services (DACOWITS)** was created in 1951 to assist with the recruitment of women. The civilian members of the committee are appointed by the president. The committee continues to function in a broad way in the 1990s, advising the Department of Defense on various matters related to women's military service.[13]

When the conflict in Korea ended in 1953, Dwight D. Eisenhower, a Republican, was serving his first term as president. The general mood in the country during the mid-1950s was fairly calm and positive, but things began to change toward the end of Eisenhower's second term in the late 1950s. National concerns included an unstable economy, a large national debt, and unsettling social problems. New concerns with foreign policy emerged when the Soviets launched a Sputnik satellite in the fall of 1957. This development indicated that the Soviets had the technology for space exploration. Such technology might lead to the launching of long-range nuclear weapons at high speeds. Fear was mounting among Americans about our nation's ability to compete with the Soviet Union in terms of the technology that might be used in warfare.

Into the 1960s

The election of John F. Kennedy to the presidency in 1960 brought a sense of hope and renewed energy to the country. Kennedy was young, handsome, an intellectual, educated at Harvard, and a war hero. His administration presented an image of dynamic youthfulness. The man and his image had a dramatic effect on young people, and many answered Kennedy's call to serve their country.

Barbara Regina Nyce was twenty-eight years old when she entered the Navy in 1962. She had a B.S. degree in education and had been teaching in a junior high school in Baltimore, Maryland. Several things influenced her decision to join the military at this time. As she put it, "[I had] a desire to respond to President John F. Kennedy's challenge to do something for my country and a dissatisfaction with teaching as a profession." While she would receive a fifty percent pay cut at the beginning, she saw some long-term benefits. Some of these were an increased salary and promotional opportunities as long as performance and potential warranted it. The military provided the challenge Barbara Nyce wanted and appeared both demanding and adventuresome, yet offered a measure of security. She describes her own experiences and those of other Navy women, in general, during the 1960s.

"In the 1960s all aspects of **basic training** were separate from men's. The content of the courses and length of time for them were different. Physical requirements during training were not very demanding, consisting of a physical education-type class about twice a week and a demonstrated ability to swim a specific distance. Although not categorized as physical training, drill classes, three or four times a week, provided a form of exercise. Women did not carry rifles during drill, but were required to learn to fire a handgun.

Academic requirements for women included basic orientation [to the structure and organization of the Navy and naval terms], and courses aimed at preparing women officers for the areas in which most of them would be assigned. Women also attended grooming courses, which included such topics as make-up application, correct posture, appropriate civilian attire, etc., and [ended] in a fashion show."

"No Clout"

After completing the initial training, Barbara was commissioned as an ensign in March 1963.

"I experienced *different* treatment [from that of men] throughout my career. From the beginning I experienced the standard treatment accorded any woman who attempted to invade the male world. In general, that included not being taken seriously, not being assigned to tasks that were as demanding as those assigned to my male counterparts, and always and repeatedly having to prove myself in each new situation or with each new boss.

Until the early 1970s all aspects of women's careers [in the military] were different from men's. Women were not recruited if they were married or had dependent children. They could not stay on active duty if they became pregnant or if they became the guardian of a child eighteen or under. Women were recruited and assigned by other women and competed for promotion only with other women. Because we were small in number, about five hundred, and segregated, many male officers served full careers without *any* association with women officers. We had no impact on their careers. We did not compete with them for assignments or for promotions, nor did we serve as voting members of the boards which considered them for promotion or for special career-enhancing assignments. In essence, we had no clout . . . We were present—but some considered us unnecessary.

Assignment for women initially was done by another woman officer, and women officers usually relieved other women officers in a 'woman's job.' There was only one command to which women could aspire—Recruit Training Command for Women—an all female staff overseeing the training of all female recruits. The types and, therefore the numbers, of jobs open to women were constrained. The justification offered was Title 10 U.S. Code Section 6015, which disallowed the permanent assignment of women to combatant vessels and aircraft. In practice, however, the law was misused to prohibit even official visits of Navy women to ships. One particularly egregious application of the law involved dependents' (wives and children) one-day cruises. Navy women who requested permission to board ships for a dependents' cruise could be authorized to take part provided they were on leave status and did not wear their uniforms [the reason for these requirements was not specified].

Pay for Navy men and women of equivalent rank is the same. However, inequities often exist because of laws affecting promotions and assignments. For example, before the 1970s women officers became eligible for promotion to lieutenant from eighteen to twenty-four months later than men. (Men who were commissioned at the same time that I was were promoted to lieutenant one year earlier than I, not because of ability, but because they were males.) That time lag resulted in less pay for women throughout their careers.

Because women were excluded by law and policy from combatant assignments, they could not earn bonuses and special pays with the same frequency, and of the same magnitude as men could. They could not serve on combatant ships (including all submarines) and aircraft. Therefore, they were not assigned to certain highly technical ratings whose sea duty is aboard these combatant units. Consequently, they could not earn any, or as much, sea pay, combat pay, responsibility pay, hazardous duty pay, submarine pay, flight pay, reenlistment bonuses, etc., as men could. On average, Navy women earn less than Navy men of equivalent rank, not because women voluntarily avoid extra pay assignments, but because they are barred by law and policy from certain of those extra pay assignments.

When I entered the Navy, women officers could aspire only to the rank of commander, the next higher rank of captain being reserved for one woman and only while she held the job of Assistant Chief of Naval Personnel for Women, informally known as Director of the WAVES. Career development for women was not as clearly defined as it was for men. Women were required to perform well in order to be promoted, but the types of jobs they held were less significant in determining their promotability. Career development for men in the unrestricted line communities required repetitive sea tours in **billets** of increasing importance and responsibility. Men whose careers included commander and captain **tours [of duty]** as commanding officers at sea could aspire to promotion to the four highest possible flag ranks. By the late 1960s, the highest rank a woman could hold permanently was captain. Legally, women officers were not eligible for promotion to the top four pay grades."

Vietnam and New Laws

Unlike the situations in World Wars I and II, the military did not actively recruit women and offer them expanded opportunities during the conflict in Vietnam. Fewer than ten thousand women served in Vietnam, the majority in nursing and other medical specialties. Even though they were not assigned to direct combat jobs, the women were exposed to combat conditions. Four Navy nurses were injured in a Vietcong terrorist bombing and were the first American women in the conflict to be awarded the Purple Heart. Eight Army nurses died in action and their names are inscribed on the Vietnam Memorial Wall in Washington, D.C. A few thousand women served in support functions, such as storekeeping, vehicle maintenance, and in administrative and clerical jobs in nearby countries.[14]

As United States military participation in Vietnam grew during the late 1960s and early 1970s, public opposition to our involvement and to the **draft** also increased. This opposition, along with pressures within society for equal treatment of racial and ethnic minorities and women, led to dramatic changes. New social programs were introduced in civilian society and changes in military policies improved the situation for military women.

A major change took place in 1967. In that year laws were passed that changed several of the provisions of the Women's Armed Services Integration Act of 1948. Limitations on the percentages of enlisted women and female officers were removed. Also removed were the inequities in retirement benefits for men and women. Some of the restrictions on career opportunities—most notably, promotion to higher ranks—were changed. Even though the new laws offered women more opportunities, they did not create complete equality of service with that of men. The 1967 laws did not dissolve separate promotion systems for men and women, for example, nor did they equalize benefits received by their dependents or allow women to enter the service academies.[15]

★ ★ ★ ★ ★ ★ ★ ★ ★ ★ ★ ★ ★ ★ ★ ★ ★ ★

CHAPTER
TWO

Gaining Ground:
The Expansion Years—
1970s and 1980s

Women's military opportunities grew dramatically during the 1970s. It was a time of profound social change. Within civilian society, the civil rights movement of the 1960s and early 1970s promoted choices and rights for *all* citizens. Women's involvement in the civil rights movement promoted activity in the women's movement, sometimes referred to as the women's liberation movement. The purpose of this social movement was to improve the political and social status of women in American society. The ultimate goal was to provide women equal opportunities with men, politically, economically, and socially.

The Equal Rights Amendment (ERA) was passed by Congress in 1972. Although it did not become law because it was not ratified by a sufficient number of states, it affected thinking about extending equal opportunities to women. National and local organizations concerned with women's rights, together with the writings of a number of outspoken women, helped bring the issues to public attention. The nation's consciousness about women's value and position in society was raised. One result was the expansion of our society's view of the appropriate roles for women. In time it became more acceptable for women to participate in various activities outside the home.

While changes were occurring in society at large, changes in the military itself were opening up greater opportunities for women. When the draft ended in 1973, men were no longer required to serve.

The military still had to meet its personnel needs, however. It turned to volunteers. With the establishment of an **all-volunteer force (AVF),** the military began to view women as a source of personnel.

More Opportunities Open Up

Along with recruiting more women in the 1970s, the armed forces expanded their possibilities for service. The training opportunities and various jobs available to women increased rapidly. Traditionally, women had worked in areas defined as "appropriate for women," such as health care, clerical specialties, and communications. Changes in the 1970s gave women the chance to enter nontraditional areas. They became mechanics, served on missile crews, and were assigned to more naval vessels, on a permanent basis. They were offered more jobs in aviation specialties. Women first wore naval aviator wings in 1973 and Army women first flew, mainly as helicopter pilots, in 1974. In 1977 the Air Force allowed women to fly certain types of planes, such as tankers, personnel and cargo transport, medical evacuation and **reconnaissance.** They were not, however, allowed to serve on aircraft that might be involved in combat. Women were also trained to use weapons, but not for direct combat.

The expansion did not stop with increased recruitment of women and new job possibilities. A number of significant changes brought about even more career opportunities for women. In the early 1970s women were for the first time allowed to enter **Reserve Officers' Training Corps (ROTC)** programs on college campuses. This was a significant change because ROTC is the major source of military officers. In 1975 women were first admitted to the Coast Guard Academy (a federal academy, rather than a military academy, since it is under the authority of the Department of Defense only in times of emergency). Women first entered the military academies—Air Force, Naval, and West Point—in 1976. The three military academies are the main source of career officers, those expected to stay in the military for a long time.

Also during the 1970s, women received promotions to the general officer ranks and served as commanders of units and organizations consisting of both men and women. The separate Women's Corps

An Army helicopter pilot at Fort Hood, Texas. Changes in the military in the 1970s opened up new, non-traditional areas to women.

were eliminated and women were integrated into all services with men. This meant that they came under the same command structure, were subject to the same standards of performance and discipline, and received equal pay and benefits. Policies restricting the service of married women and requiring the discharge of pregnant women and those with children under eighteen were done away with.[1]

Equal Opportunity

Efforts by the Department of Defense and the separate armed services contributed to the further expansion of opportunities for military women in the 1980s. Early in the decade the DoD released a statement expressing its intention to provide women equal opportunity with men in all areas of military service in which women's participation was not prohibited by combat exclusion laws and policies.

Barriers to women had begun to fall. Now all branches of the

29

service offered women new possibilities. For example, Air Force women could join the crews of more aircraft, including those with spy and surveillance missions. They could also serve on two-person missile crews for the Minuteman and Patriot missile systems. At first, women could only work with other women on these crews because of concerns about problems with "stress and privacy" that might occur if women and men had to work together in confined and isolated settings. In 1988 women were assigned to mixed gender crews. Another nontraditional area, security jobs, was also opened to Air Force women at this time.

Barriers to women began to fall in other branches of the services. The Army opened numerous positions to women on missile crews, in units closer to the battlefront, and in peacekeeping forces. The Marine Corps offered women training opportunities in new areas, including battle skills and survival and defensive combat operations. Women marines were first allowed to choose jobs in the security area, including security-guard positions in selected locations overseas. The Marines Corps continued to reserve the right to send men to "hardship" security posts on bases and at embassies in foreign countries. ("Hardship" is defined by the military as a dangerous or harsh environment for women. The local customs and treatment of women continue to influence this determination.)

Navy women were offered many choices of assignments to ships—choices that had previously been closed to them. The biggest gain, in terms of sea assignment, came in 1988 when ships in the combat logistics force were opened to women. This allowed them to serve on ships that traveled with the battle group—close to areas where combat might take place. Women also were selected to command sea vessels for the first time.[2]

Getting Some Clout

Barbara Nyce reflects upon her experience in the Navy during this expansion period.

"External pressure from the civilian women's movement forced the military to modify many of its policies with respect to women. From the early 1970s to the early 1980s monumental strides were made in integrating women into the Navy's mainstream. At both the captain and commander level women were assigned to command ashore with staffs that included both men and women. Women were routinely sent to prestigious **War College** assignments as students and were assigned to high visibility jobs of significant responsibility such as Deputy to the Assistant Chief of Naval Personnel, Executive Secretary to the Chairman of the Joint Chiefs of Staff (JCS), [and] commanding officers of technical schools and initial training schools. Women became acknowledged experts in an assortment of specialty fields and often were sought out by their seniors because of their expertise. All career fields were opened to women, with the exception of submarine duty and those enlisted ratings having the bulk of their jobs aboard combatant ships.

The most significant change to women's status came from the enactment of the **Defense Officer Personnel Management Act (DOPMA)** in 1980. [This act] resulted in the Navy's assigning women officers to officer promotion boards considering both men and women for promotion. We were beginning to get some clout!"

While Barbara recognizes that the official integration of women into the military offered them many opportunities, inequalities still existed. She observes the continued existence of a "generalist" community in the Navy:[3]

"Cosmetically integrated, in reality [this generalist community] remains a women's community tied together by its lack of sea duty. Over eighty-five percent of the generalist community are women and its unofficial head is a woman admiral. The only generalist officers with career potential are women. Top quality male officers are not going to be satisfied with a career ashore."

Since the Navy's main concern is with service at sea, shore assignments do not have as much status as sea assignments.

Barbara points out other examples of the remaining inequalities:

"Women will continue to be viewed as substitutes for unavailable men, instead of being valued for their talents, abilities, and contributions. Although eligibility for promotion to admiral is the same for men and women, the number of women line admirals remains

31

constant at two. Almost magically, a woman is selected for admiral at about the same time another woman admiral retires."[4]

Changing Attitudes and Conditions

In the late 1980s the DoD created a task force to study issues related to women's military service. Three issues were identified as important to pursue: (1) attitudes toward military women and the effect of these attitudes on morale and the quality of life; (2) the effect of personnel policies on women's career development; and (3) the consistency of the services' use of the combat exclusion laws and policies and their impact on women's assignments.

The DoD responded to the recommendations made by the task force by directing the services to work on improving conditions for women in several areas. These areas included sexual harassment, the availability of appropriate recreational facilities and entertainment, and the offering of adequate medical care for women's health needs. As for career development, the services attempted to give women better preparation for leadership and more opportunities to be assigned to important positions. These positions would include command assignments.

The recommendations of the task force that related to the services' use of combat exclusion laws and policies in the assignment of women had the most dramatic impact on women's opportunities. The task force noted the lack of uniformity in the assignment of women among the various branches of the service. In order to create consistency in assignment procedures across the services, the DoD provided a standard definition of "combat" and directed the services to use a **"Risk Rule"** to determine the positions available to women. This resulted in opening over thirty thousand positions in the active-duty and reserve forces for women.[5]

How does the general public react to the idea of women in combat? In the past, the general public seemed to believe that women in the United States military were not exposed to risk because of protection by combat exclusion laws and policies. This is not true. As noted in Chapter 1, women have been exposed to great risk during all the wars they have been involved in, officially or unofficially. They have been captured as prisoners of war and some have lost their lives.

Historical evidence supports this conclusion, as does women's participation in United States military activities during the 1980s. Air Force women served on air crews that airlifted troops and supplies during the invasion of Grenada in 1983 and the air raid in Libya in 1986. Women in the Army performed various duties in support of the efforts in Grenada.[6] Approximately 800 Army women took part in the United States invasion of Panama in 1989 and an estimated 150 women might have been in areas where fighting took place. Two women who piloted helicopters that delivered troops to hostile areas received medals.

During the invasion of Panama, Captain Linda Bray became the center of controversy about women in combat. She had troops exposed to hostile fire on three different occasions during the invasion and had ordered her company into battle against a Panamanian Defense Force position. Although Bray and the other women performed jobs that took them into hostile areas, they were not *officially* assigned to direct combat positions. Their involvement, therefore, did not violate combat exclusion laws or policies.[7] This is an example of how the military interprets and uses laws and policies to assign women in ways that most benefit the needs of the military.

CHAPTER
THREE

Women's Current Service in the Military

As we mentioned in the introduction, the Department of Defense has authority over the Air Force, Army, Navy, and Marines. The Coast Guard is under the direction of the Department of Transportation during peacetime, but is responsible to the Department of Defense (Navy) in time of war. Official DoD policy expresses a commitment to equal treatment of women and men in all areas to which women may be assigned. The combat exclusion laws and policies mentioned in earlier chapters determine the areas available to women. It is important to remember that decisions about assigning women are not always clearly defined. They are sometimes based on the military's subjective interpretation of the law.

Information published by the DoD in September 1992 indicated that 208,398 women were serving on active duty in the United States military (including the Coast Guard). An additional 148,785 women were in the reserves. Women also serve in National Guard units in the Army and Air Force.[1] Under usual circumstances, these units are under the direction of the separate states, but they may be activated and come under federal control during war, as was the case during the Persian Gulf War in 1991.

By Branch

The information about the percentages and types of jobs available to women in each of the branches describes the situation in the early 1990s. On April 28, 1993, the Secretary of Defense, Les Aspin, issued an order to lift the ban on women in combat aviation jobs. He also

In the 1980s the Air Force allowed women to join mixed crews in a variety of aircraft. This navigator of a Stratotanker checks her charts while on a fueling flight.

directed the Navy to begin increasing women's assignments on ships. He will ask Congress to repeal the law which bars women from serving on combat ships. It is the only remaining combat exclusion law from 1948. Aspin also ordered the services to review and justify the exclusion of women from the remaining combat jobs. While the order is to be put into effect immediately, it will take awhile for the services to select and train women for the newly opened jobs. It is estimated that more than 20,000 jobs on planes and ships will be opened to women over time. These jobs have previously been held by men only and are important for promotion to the highest military ranks.[2] This 1993 order will be discussed more fully in Chapter 7.

As of early 1990, 97 percent of the jobs in the Air Force were open to women. Of all the services, the Air Force has the highest percentage of women (14.7) on active duty. Women make up 19 percent of the reserves. This higher percentage is related to the fact that the Air Force offers women more job opportunities than do the other services.[3]

Air Force women currently serve in all officer career fields. They have not been assigned to aircraft that take part in combat operations behind enemy lines because of the combat exclusions stated in the 1948 legislation mentioned in Chapter 1. In December, 1991 President George Bush signed the **National Defense Authorization Act for Fiscal Years 1992 and 1993.** The act included congressional repeal of the 1948 law that barred women from flying planes on combat missions. But this repeal did not require the Air Force to assign women to combat aircraft; rather, it *allowed* the service to make the decision.

The 1991 legislation also established a presidential commission to study the assignment of women in the armed forces. A Department of Defense spokesman reported that the **Pentagon** would not assign any women to combat aircraft until the commission made its recommendations. In November 1992 the commission voted eight to seven to recommend that the services continue to *prohibit* women from flying combat aircraft. Members of the commission agreed that women are capable of flying these planes, but those who voted to keep the ban were concerned that female pilots might interfere with the cohesion among male pilots. They were also concerned about the possibility of women pilots being shot down and taken as prisoners of war.[4]

Even though some senior military officials shared the commission's concerns, the Secretary of Defense lifted the ban on women in combat aviation. Air Force women will now be allowed to compete with men for these jobs. Seven women have been selected for fighter pilot training and more will soon be offered the opportunity. Lieutenant Jeanne Flynn graduated first in her pilot training class but was turned down for fighter pilot training because of the combat exclusion practices. Now she will be the first female fighter pilot in the Air Force.[5]

Enlisted women in the Air Force have been able to choose from all but four specialties. They were *excluded* from combat control, tactical command and control, aerial gunner, and para-rescue and recovery.[6] Some jobs in these specialty areas are likely to open as a result of the new assignment policies.

As we mentioned earlier, policies, rather than laws, limit the service of Army women. In the early 1990s they were able to serve in 52 percent of the jobs in the Army. More opportunities will be available as the newly announced changes are put into effect. For example, women will pilot Apache and Cobra helicopters and might be assigned to field artillery and air defense combat units. Women make up 12.2 percent of the active-duty strength and 20.6 percent of the reserve forces.

The Navy is actively recruiting women to serve in a variety of nontraditional jobs. Women have been allowed to choose from 59 percent of the positions in the Navy. They make up 10.4 percent of the active-duty strength and 15.1 percent of the reserves.[7]

In the past few years Navy women have had more opportunities than they once had to serve in sea-duty assignments and aviation specialties such as piloting aircraft and commanding aviation squadrons. A few female pilots have served as instructors and test pilots for fighter planes and some women have been allowed to fly them in training exercises. While these women have demonstrated their capabilities, they have not been allowed to fly the same planes in combat because of the exclusion laws and policies. This will soon change as a result of the recent lifting of these restrictions.[8] Female pilots are excited about their new opportunities.

The presidential commission recommended that women be allowed to serve on combat vessels, except submarines and **amphibious vessels.** In order for the Navy to follow this recommendation, the 1948 law which excludes women from combatant vessels would have to be repealed. The Secretary of Defense announced that he will ask Congress to repeal the law.[9]

Women marines have more limited opportunities than do women in the other services. Only 20 percent of the jobs have been open to women marines. More positions will be available, including aviation jobs. The Marine Corps is the only branch which has not allowed women to serve in any aviation slots. The corps has the smallest

37

percentage of women (4.7) on active duty and in the reserves (3.6).[10] The combat exclusion laws apply most strictly to women marines because of the corps' basic mission. It is an expeditionary force in readiness. This means that the marines are most likely to be sent to combat areas and be involved in ground combat when fighting occurs. In the summer of 1992 the marines announced that female officers would be given full combat training, including live firing of M-16 rifles and grenades.[11]

As we noted earlier, the Coast Guard is under the authority of the United States Department of Transportation *except* in time of war. Its major mission is to protect the United States coastline and inland waterways. Since combat involvement is not a part of the usual mission, Coast Guard women have the largest choice of jobs. All jobs are open to women. They make up 7.4 percent of the active-duty personnel and 11.3 percent of the Coast Guard Reserves.[12]

The following is a general discussion of several conditions related to women's current service in the military. It is important to remember that there will be some variations. These variations are related to the specific branch of service, the geographic location of training and assignments, and the actual persons involved. And of course, we must consider the differences between the experiences of women and men.

Recruitment

Recruitment standards used by the military are essentially the same for women and men. Educational level, mental aptitude, physical measures (height, weight, and some performance criteria), and background information are considered for both. With the exception of physical measures standards are *officially* the same for women and men. Female enlistees are more likely than males to be high school graduates.

Recruiters get the firsthand view of all those who are interested in joining the military. They meet the folks who walk in off the street. Sergeant Mike Chezek tells of his experience as a Marine recruiter in Baltimore, Maryland:

"Not too many women walk in this office. There is a stigma about it. We don't actively prospect for women so much because of some past experiences. We've had a lot of discharges from ladies who've changed their minds for one reason or another. But if we find a lady through phone calls or **canvassing** or who walks in and meets the requirements, we're more than happy to enlist a lady in the Marine Corps."

When asked about possible reasons women might enlist, Sergeant Chezek offered the following observation: "Seems like you see a girl that comes in . . . she wants to get out on her own more, she's looking for independence. Not that they're being rebellious but they seem to want to learn how to take care of themselves some. That's the impression I get from the ladies we talk to." He admitted that there are a variety of factors that motivate both women and men to think about enlisting in the military. "It's hard to characterize what the reasons are that anybody joins," he said.

Basic Training

Sergeant Chezek says that the biggest obstacle for women is likely to be basic training, or boot camp, as it is commonly called. As a part of the screening process, potential recruits see a video of basic training. Some women decide not to enlist after viewing it. He admits that some men also change their minds:

"The ladies seem to be less afraid of the stuff than men! You get a guy in here, he's a big football player, a big bruiser. Maybe he's been put on a pedestal most of his life. When he finds out there's somebody that doesn't care where he's from and is going to treat him like he's mainstream, that's going to damage an eighteen-year-old's ego. The ladies are more down to earth, basically, at that age. They come in here and they are a lot easier to deal with."

The specific content and structure of basic training varies by service. Differences in men's and women's experiences are more likely to be found in basic training rather than in job-specialty training. Enlisted persons go through a basic-training course that is different from that of officers. For example, there is more variation in content of training for enlisted men and women than for officers. The typical basic-training course for officers is similar for men and women, except that women do not receive as much instruction in combat skills.

Women usually perform the same physical activities as men, but the requirements are adjusted for physical differences. For example, women may run a shorter distance in a designated period of time or be given more time to climb a wall. Women hang from a bar for a period of time, while men do pullups. Near the end of basic training, women run in formation for three miles, while the distance for men is five miles.

Sergeant Chezek explains some of the differences in basic training for women marines: "For the ladies basic training is longer than for men because they [the women] do more weapons training [because women do not receive the extended combat skills training that men undergo]. Men will do basic warrior training in boot camp. After they leave basic training, they have to go to a twenty-eight-day combat training. The women will go straight to their **MOS school**." The abbreviation MOS stands for Military Occupational Specialty, or the job a person will perform. The content of this training is the same for men and women for all jobs that women may choose.

When asked for any reason why a woman might choose the Marines rather than one of the other services, Sergeant Chezek responded in the following way:

"We stress more discipline, physical fitness, and belonging. I think that means a lot to a young lady. I feel that boot camp experience in the Marine Corps is going to teach you more about yourself than any other service. You never are going to get anything better than the way we teach you discipline. We take care of our own. We have Marines, males and females, come in here all the time, needing help on something. We try to help them out the best we can. The Marine Corps is a small organization, a family."

Up Through the Ranks

Since the Department of Defense has a policy that provides equal opportunity for all personnel, consistent with the combat exclusion laws and policies, women compete equally with men for promotions. Overall, they are promoted at a rate similar to that of men. Women's chances for command positions are fewer, however, because combat

During boot camp recruits are molded into soldiers by their drill instructor. D.I. Sandra Nails uses the "voice" to discipline a recruit.

exclusion laws and policies bar them from certain assignments. Further, women serve in occupations that have fewer command positions, and few women are senior enough to compete for command assignments.

A 1988 government report concluded that women's career progression is a concern, but not a problem. The report noted that the combat exclusion laws and policies are probably the greatest obstacle to women's career development.[13] How and if the military handles this obstacle remains to be seen.

In the Persian Gulf War

The military's dependence on women's service was demonstrated in 1991 when United States troops were sent to the Persian Gulf. Approximately thirty-seven thousand women served in the Gulf region. It was estimated that women made up about 6.8 percent of the troops sent there. Women's involvement in the Persian Gulf War was extensive in terms of numbers and the variety of positions in which they served. In addition to the traditional medical, administrative, and communications jobs, they served as pilots and crew members of several types of aircraft (planes and helicopters), in artillery and transportation units, and on support and repair ships. They also patrolled the borders and managed prisoner of war camps. Many of these jobs were in key combat support positions and in the front lines. The performance of some duties required women to be behind enemy lines. For example, some women flew supplies and personnel into dangerous areas, while others served as crew members of medical evacuation aircraft. Women also transported supplies, such as fuel for tanks, into Iraq before the tanks moved into the area.

All of the armed services sent women to the Gulf. About twenty-six thousand Army women went to the Middle East. They took part in the initial invasion of Kuwait and Iraq and served with Patriot missile crews in Israel, Saudi Arabia, and Turkey. They commanded units of both men and women and of various sizes.

The Navy sent thirty-seven hundred women to the Gulf. In addition to performing the more traditional jobs, they piloted

A Navy enlisted woman on guard in Saudi Arabia during the Persian Gulf War. The American public first became aware of the extent of women's involvement in the military during this conflict.

helicopters and reconnaissance aircraft, served on air crews and aboard various types of ships.

About twenty-two hundred female marines served in the region, mainly in traditional jobs. They were the first female marines to travel to a combat area since the Vietnam conflict.

Approximately fifty-three hundred Air Force women were in the Gulf region. These numbers included women on active duty and in the reserves. (Chapter 4 describes the difference between these service choices.) They piloted and served on crews of transport, reconnaissance, airlift, and tanker planes. They also performed a variety of support functions.

Thirteen Coast Guard women served in **Port Security** positions. (The Coast Guard was under the authority of the Navy during the war and its personnel was sent to the area of conflict along with members of the other armed services.)

A total of thirteen women died in the Persian Gulf War, four from hostile causes and nine from nonhostile causes. Twenty-one women were wounded in action and sixteen experienced nonbattle injuries. Two Army women were taken as prisoners of war. Specialist Melissa Rathburn-Nealy was held hostage for thirty-four days after the truck in which she was riding with a male soldier was stopped by Iraqis. She reported that she was treated fairly well. Major Rhonda L. Cornum, an Army flight surgeon, was on a rescue mission looking for a downed pilot. She was captured when her helicopter crashed. Five of the crew members were killed. Major Cornum broke both arms and injured her legs in the crash. She was treated harshly and sexually molested by Iraqi soldiers. Both women received the same three medals that were awarded to male prisoners of war.[14] Major Cornum later wrote of her war experiences. In her book, *She Went to War*, Cornum suggests that too much attention may be focused on the treatment of female prisoners of war. She believes that male prisoners were mistreated as much as, if not more than, the women prisoners.

One Woman's Story

Numerous **National Guard** units were sent to the Gulf region during the conflict there. Many women made up these units and experienced war firsthand.

Sergeant Marie Elliott entered the National Guard in 1979, three years after graduating from high school. She currently serves in the 290th Military Police unit of the Army National Guard in Maryland. Before joining the guard she worked as a waitress.

Sergeant Elliott's unit was called to active duty in 1990 and sent to the Persian Gulf late that year. This is how Marie Elliott recalls her experiences in the Gulf:

"The unit was activated on the 15th of November 1990 and on the 17th we went to Fort Meade, Maryland, for training. We did a lot of marching and weapons qualifications. Everyone had to qualify with their weapons. There was a lot of NBC (nuclear, biological, and chemical) warfare training.

How did I feel at first? I had a TV reporter ask me that and I couldn't answer him. Scared—I was scared. My family was more

Sergeant Marie Elliott

scared than I was. But I knew I was going to go. There was no way that I was going to try to come up with a reason to get out of it. Because like I said, I had been in eleven years and you feel a sense of commitment after awhile."

The unit left Maryland on a commercial airline on December 10 and arrived in Saudi Arabia on December 11, 1990.

"The majority of the time we were there [in Saudi Arabia] we stayed in tents. When we first got to our location it was crowded, but then more tents became available so people could spread out more."

Assignment to tents was based on jobs, so men and women shared the same tents. Privacy was not a concern because the tents were divided so that each person had his or her own section.

"At first we had to bathe in big plastic buckets. Later we did get shower stalls, three showers in each stall. We'd fill them up with water and then put signs on the door, male or female. Usually when a female went to take a shower, another female went with her or a male would go as a guard. You stood in the shower stall and you had to reach up to turn the water on and it would come right down on your head. The shower facilities were probably the biggest inconvenience.

You had to wash your clothing. It had to all be done by hand and hung up to dry. We washed everything out in buckets and hung it out on a clothesline. We did have an iron, but we didn't iron anything. They had a generator and each tent had lighting and a way to plug in something if you needed to.

The meals we ate were MREs (meals ready to eat). If you can heat them up, they're not too bad. We were given kerosene heaters. You could add a little water to the MRE and heat it up. They were tolerable. Most of the time we had at least one hot meal a day. Our cooks did an outstanding job the whole time we were there.

Medical facilities were available. We usually had people on sick call each morning, for whatever reason: colds, headaches, toothaches, whatever. If it was something more serious, that they couldn't handle, then [the person was] transported to an evacuation hospital. Everybody got the medical treatment they needed.

We kept up with the news by radio—the Armed Forces Radio Network. It was on all the time. When the air war started, that's all you heard for, maybe four days solid. When the ground war started, it was the same thing. Of course, it didn't last four days. We were made aware of everything that was happening with that.

We did get quite a bit of mail on a regular basis; everybody wrote. We sent out tons of mail each day because we got quite a bit of mail. We did make phone calls while we were there. It was usually about once a week. The phones were usually within twenty to forty minutes drive. I called home a total of four times while I was over there, collect from Saudi Arabia.

They had religious ceremonies on a weekly basis, all different religions, in a chapel tent. If anyone had a problem they needed to talk to the Reverend about, they could go and talk."

In some Middle Eastern cultures, women are expected to conform to traditional roles. Their dress is restrictive; their arms, legs, hair, and faces are covered. In some countries, women are not allowed to drive automobiles. The American military was concerned about the response of the Saudis to the dress and activities of American women, who enjoy much greater freedom in the United States. There were reports of Saudi criticism of women who did not cover their bodies properly, as defined by local customs, and of those who drove military vehicles. Overall, it seems that some type of compromise between Americans and Saudis was reached. The arrangements varied from one military unit to another and also depended on the country in which the unit was stationed.

Sergeant Elliott did not personally experience many problems as a woman, but she admits that she did not have much interaction with the local people: "If they'd see a female driving a vehicle, they'd look, but . . . I don't think anything was said. If your sleeves were rolled up, they'd *really* look at you!"

Sergeant Elliott said that she did not feel that female soldiers had more problems than males serving in the Gulf region: "If there was something negative, I think that it was negative for both males and females. I wouldn't say that one thing was negative for one and not the other. It was pretty much kept equal."

The Military Police unit in which Sergeant Elliott served was not in an area where they could see the air war, but they could hear the bombs, in the distance, in the evening. She describes her feelings while she was in the area:

"I wouldn't classify it as being afraid, but you were always aware of what was going on around you. You were very cautious of whatever you did.

The hardest thing about being there was being away from your family. Being in the field, I don't consider a problem. I've been in the unit for a long time and I enjoy going to the field, because it's different than what I'm doing everyday. This was a little longer than I expected, but it was different. It was an experience I'll never forget. It had its good points, its bad points, its ups and downs."

According to Sergeant Elliott, there were several good things about serving in the Gulf:

"Self-satisfaction. You know that you were there for a purpose and that you were doing something you were sent there for. It gave you a sense of pride . . . that you went somewhere with a group of people and you did something. When you work closely with a group of people it can be very stressful at times. Stressful just for the fact that you're with someone in close quarters for that length of time. But there's a purpose behind it. It's to get a mission done and you just have to remember that."

Some Results of the Persian Gulf War

Captain Carol Barkalow graduated from West Point in 1980, the first graduating class that included women. In a May 1991 article in The *New York Times,* she made the following observations: "Until the Persian Gulf the American people didn't understand the modern battlefield. Even in noncombat roles, women have been exposed to risk for some time."

Captain Barkalow believes that male officers' attitudes toward women changed when they saw how well women performed in the Gulf.

"Many of the guys of my generation have had the experience [of working with women as peers] but the senior military ranks have *never* worked with women as peers. Someone twenty years my senior and a general still sees women as a mother, wife, girlfriend, or daughter. They know how to deal with guys but may not know what to do with women. It makes them uncomfortable."

When General H. Norman Schwarzkopf (United States Army), commander of the Allied Forces in the Gulf, was interviewed on the ABC News program "20/20" on March 22, 1991, he had this to say about women's performance in the war:

"You know the percentage of women in the Army is about 12.5 percent and they are absolutely indispensable. They did a magnificent job out there. There were all sorts of jobs that were done by women. You know, you got to be proud of women in the service, just like I'm proud of the men in the service. I mean, their performance was terrific."

Children Left Behind—Not Just a Woman's Issue

Women's involvement in the Gulf War attracted considerable attention and generated controversy about their military participation. The media often called it the "Mom's War" because many women who went to the region left children behind. Images on television and in magazines showed military women saying goodbye to their young children. Many people viewed children being left behind as a woman's issue. It would be more accurate to think of it as a parent's issue.

Service men are more likely to be married and have children than are service women. There are male soldiers on active duty who are single parents with custody of minor children. Very little, if anything, was mentioned about military fathers leaving their children. Also, there are many joint-service couples who have young children. Anytime the United States sends troops away from home, it is possible that both parents who are service members will be sent.

The Department of Defense is aware of the problems that might arise when one or both parents are called away from home for military duty. To avoid last-minute problems, single parents and joint-service couples are required to have a dependent care plan that specifies custody arrangements for children under eighteen in the event of the parents' **deployment.** These plans seem to have worked well in recent situations that have required United States forces to travel to areas of conflict. The Gulf situation was somewhat different because it involved such a large number of active troops and the largest mobilization of reserves since the Korean conflict. Problems with the care of dependents seem to be greater for people in the reserves because they are less accustomed to being sent away from home than are service members on active duty.[15]

What to do with the children is clearly an issue that needs attention, and DoD family policy needs refinement. One should remember that this is a personnel issue, not just a woman's issue, and a family policy should apply equally to male and female single parents and members of joint-service couples.

Women did all kinds of jobs during the war in the Persian Gulf, from flying helicopters to loading supplies. Some were wounded and taken prisoner and some died.

Public Reaction to Women in the Gulf

During the Gulf crisis, Americans expressed a range of emotions—shock, horror, resignation, and pride—when facing the possibility of women being killed in action or taken prisoners of war. Some reacted with anger when they heard how close women were to the front lines, especially since they are considered noncombatants. Others, including parents of daughters in the region, expressed concern but felt that women should be given equal opportunity.

Military women who were interviewed by the newspaper and television reporters assigned to cover the conflict tried to downplay the fact that they were women. They emphasized that they wanted to be treated as soldiers with a job to do. One of these was Major Marie Rossi, who was one of the first women to fly a helicopter behind enemy lines. In an interview on CNN, she commented: "I think if you talk to the women who are professionals in the military, we see ourselves as soldiers. We don't really see it as man versus woman." A couple of days after the interview, Major Rossi died when her helicopter hit a microwave tower. She was buried in Arlington National Cemetery, with full military honors.

In a February 1, 1991, interview on "CBS This Morning," Pat Foote, who retired from the Army at the rank of brigadier general, suggested that overconcern with women's situations might prevent them from performing jobs for which they are trained. She also recognized the tendency of the public and the military to overreact to the taking of the first female prisoner of war in the Gulf. This was not the first time an American woman had been captured by the enemy, Foote observed. Approximately eighty women were taken prisoner in World War II and they all came home alive. General Foote supported the lifting of all combat restrictions for military women.

The importance of women's contributions in the Gulf initiated changes in their military opportunities. These changes are reflected in the 1991 legislation removing the legal ban on their service in combat aviation and the recent order to open more combat jobs to women.

In recent years Americans have expressed more favorable views of women being assigned to more military jobs. Women's performance in the Gulf convinced the public that women could and *should* be allowed to do more. Even though we say that women are not assigned to direct combat jobs, it is now clear that they perform many duties that expose them to risk of injury, capture, and death.

The Roper Organization conducted a public-opinion survey for the presidential commission in 1992. Results indicated that the public is about evenly split when asked about assigning women to direct combat in general. However, when asked about assignment to specific combat jobs, the majority of those interviewed approved of women being assigned to combat aircraft and combatant vessels but *not* to ground combat jobs or units. About half of those who supported women in combat said they should be assigned to these jobs only if they volunteer.[16]

Women in Other Militaries

How do the military opportunities of American women compare with those of women in the armed forces of our allies in NATO? In some ways the United States has been viewed as the leader in the integration of women into the military. This assessment has been based on the fact that the number and percentage of women in our military are larger than those in the armed forces of the other NATO countries.

The United States is not the leader, however, if you consider the variety of positions available to women. In Belgium, Canada, Denmark, and Norway, women may be assigned to *any* position, including combat, for which they meet the qualifications. British women may serve on combatant ships and in combat aircraft, but not in ground combat units. All combat assignments, except submarines and the Marine Corps, are open to women in the Dutch armed forces.[17]

While more possibilities exist for military women in these countries, large numbers have not yet been assigned to combat jobs. In part this is because the policies are fairly new and not many women have completed the required training. It is also the case that women who might be interested in the positions do not meet the physical requirements for the jobs, especially in ground combat units. Those opposed to offering American military women similar expanded opportunities point out that the armed forces in these countries are not as likely as the United States military to be involved in combat not as likely as the United States military to be involved in combat operations. This is because the United States has a central role in the United Nations and has official agreements with more foreign nations to help protect and defend their interests.

Israel is not a member of NATO, but is one of our important allies in the Middle East. The Israeli military has interesting, and often misunderstood, policies regarding women in the Israeli Defense Force (IDF). Like men, women are subject to a two-year period of military service when they reach the age of eighteen. Even though military service is legally required of women, fewer Israeli women than men are drafted. There are several reasons for this. The law has been modified several times since it was adopted in 1949, and some of the modifications have specified a number of **deferments** and **exemptions** for women. For example, married women, mothers (even if not married) of small children, and women with strong religious convictions are not required to serve. Women who are accepted by a college may be deferred, but are required to fulfill the obligation after they complete their education. The personnel needs of the IDF also determine how many women are drafted.

There is a widespread myth regarding Israeli women's participation in combat operations. This may partly be associated with their involvement in early military activities prior to the formation of the state of Israel. Also, the 1960 film *Exodus* probably did a lot to fuel the myth. The fact is, however, that while women in the IDF are assigned to combat units, they most certainly are not assigned to combat jobs and do not go into battle with their units. Instead, they perform a variety of support jobs for the men in the units. Since 1943 the IDF policy has been to keep women out of combat operations.[18]

CHAPTER
FOUR

Choices for Service: Branches, Active Duty, Reserves, and National Guard

If you are thinking about joining the military, you have several decisions to make. First you should think about which branch, or service, you might be interested in joining. You also should consider whether you want to join the military on a full-time or part-time basis. A brief description of the various branches of the armed forces and the choices related to full- or part-time service is presented in this chapter. The discussion in Chapter 3 of women's current service in the military will also provide useful information for helping you decide.

Still another decision has to be made regarding whether you will join the officer or enlisted ranks. These options are described in Chapters 5 and 6. More specific information on ranks, pay grades, and qualifications can be found in the tables beginning on page 131 and may also be obtained from your high school guidance counselors and local military recruiters.

An Overview of the Branches

If you like to fly or think you would like to work in some area of aviation, you might want to consider joining the Air Force, since it is the main aerospace branch of the United States military. The Air Force is the youngest branch of the American armed forces. It was formed as a separate service in 1947. Before then it was part of the Army and was known as the Army Air Corps. The Air Force's mission of protecting and defending the interests of the United States and its allies is performed with the help of some of the most advanced technology in the world. Air Force pilots fly various types of aircraft, including long-range bombers, fighters, Airborne Warning and Control Systems Aircraft (AWACS), helicopters, and space shuttles. Female pilots may fly several types of aircraft, but have not been assigned to combat aviation jobs. This will soon change since the Secretary of Defense ordered the services to assign women to fly combat aircraft. Seven women have been chosen to become combat pilots and soon more will be selected.[1]

In addition to flying, members of the Air Force perform numerous jobs that support flying missions, such as jobs in maintenance and repair, air traffic control, health care, and administration. Still other jobs involve gathering intelligence data and firefighting. Air Force bases are located around the world.[2]

If you prefer to spend most of your time on land, you might think about joining the Army. The Army has a long history, rooted in the early militia system inherited from the British. Its mission of protecting and defending the interests of the United States and its allies is carried out through land-based operations all over the world. The work of the Army is carried out by a team of soldiers (enlisted personnel, or **enlistees**), **noncommissioned officers (NCOs)** and **commissioned officers.** Army men and women work in many types of jobs in such areas as administration, health care, and operation and maintenance of vehicles, aircraft, weapons, and technical electronic systems.[3]

Some people love being around the water, for recreation or for work. If you are one who loves the sea and enjoys water activities, consider joining the Navy. This branch of the armed forces plays an important role in maintaining freedom of the seas. It protects the rights of the United States and its allies to travel and trade freely on oceans throughout the world. The Navy provides both sea and air power to protect and defend these interests. Naval officers and sailors (enlisted persons) serve on ships at sea, including submarines, in aviation jobs on land and sea, and on shore bases in many foreign countries. They perform various duties in such areas as administration, operation and repair of ships and aircraft, communications, law, medicine, intelligence, and engineering.

The Marine Corps, the smallest branch of the United States

military, is under the supervision of the Department of the Navy. Its mission is somewhat unique compared to those of the other services. The corps serves as an expeditionary force in readiness. This means that the marines are prepared to respond quickly to protect the interests and commitments of the United States anywhere in the world. Marines are often the first military personnel to be sent to areas of conflict.

Marines serve on naval ships and as security guards at United States embassies in other countries, at the White House and presidential retreat at Camp David, and at the National Security Agency. They perform many others jobs, including piloting planes and helicopters, driving armored vehicles, gathering intelligence information, and maintaining and repairing vehicles, aircraft, weapons, and equipment. The United States Marine Corps is one of the most elite fighting forces in the world.[4]

Another possibility for people who like to be around water, but who want to stay close to the United States, is the Coast Guard. You may recall that this branch of the service is under the Department of Transportation during peacetime. Its mission is to protect America's coastlines and inland waterways. Responsibilities include enforcement of customs and fishing laws, combating drug smuggling, conducting search and rescue missions, and maintaining lighthouses and other navigational aids. Members also protect marine wildlife, fight pollution in waterways and along coastlines, monitor harbor traffic, and promote boating safety. A wide variety of choices of occupations is available to support the Coast Guard's mission. As you may recall from Chapter 3, there are no restrictions on the assignment of Coast Guard women. *All* jobs are open, including the command of vessels. Since the Coast Guard is under the authority of the DoD during wartime, members have participated in all major United States military involvements.[5]

Prior to 1973 men were drafted into the military. Since that time, military service has been totally voluntary. When a person volunteers to join the military, he or she agrees to serve for a certain period of time, which is known as the **service obligation.** The specific time required by the service obligation varies, depending on the branch and program chosen by the volunteer. The following is a general overview of one's full-time and part-time service options.

Active Duty

Full-time military service is known as active duty. When persons serve on active duty, they are responsible to their service twenty-four hours a day, seven days a week. The duties associated with most military jobs can be performed in a forty-hour week, like most jobs in the civilian labor force. Sometimes, during emergencies or training exercises, for example, service members may work additional hours, including weekends. When this happens, active-duty members do *not* receive overtime pay or compensation hours. Active-duty service requires a full-time commitment without extra compensation. In general, people who wish to join the active-duty military must meet citizenship, physical, mental aptitude, educational, and moral requirements. Age standards vary from one branch of the service to another.

Reserves

Reserve forces make up an important part of the American military. Reserve units support the mission of the full-time, active-duty military by providing trained personnel to meet the expanded needs of the regular services during times of national emergency. The reserves also perform a variety of support activities during peacetime. The reserves consist of seven different forces—the Air Force, Army, Navy, Marine Corps, and Coast Guard Reserves and the Air Force and Army National Guard. Applicants to the reserves must meet standards similar to those required of persons who volunteer for active-duty service. Some members who leave the active-duty force remain in the reserves after completing their full-time service obligation.

Initially, reservists serve on active duty for several months while they complete basic- and job-training courses. For the rest of their service obligation, they perform military duties on a part-time basis. This usually consists of one or two days each month (evenings or weekends) and one period of active duty (usually from ten to fourteen days) each year.

Reservists usually work on a full-time basis in the civilian world. Many hold military jobs that offer them an interesting and exciting change from their usual work. Others serve in military career fields that are similar to their regular jobs. In both cases, reservists agree that their military training and experience improve their skills and qualities important for success in civilian life.[6]

In times of national emergency, reservists may be called to active duty for an indefinite period of time. In the United States involvement in the Persian Gulf, several reserve units were activated. Some units were sent to the Gulf region and others were assigned to United States bases at home as replacements for active-duty members sent overseas.

National Guard

The unique organization of the Army and Air National Guard includes a dual mission. The guard is a part of the reserve arm of the Army and Air Force and is under federal control during national emergencies. During peacetime, guard units have state missions. They provide disaster relief and maintain peace and order during times of civil unrest. For example, Florida National Guard units assisted victims of Hurricane Andrew in 1992. The same year, guard units in California helped maintain order and protect properties from looters during the Los Angeles riots. In both of these circumstances the units were under state authority.

After a minimum of twelve weeks of active duty for basic- and job-training, guard members, like other reservists, have a part-time military commitment. They usually hold civilian jobs and perform military duties two days each month and approximately two continuous weeks each year.

Numerous job opportunities are offered to members of the guard. They are eligible for advanced-training schools and promotions in rank. Educational assistance and retirement benefits are also available.[7]

Service in the National Guard: A Personal Account

Technical Sergeant Deborah Strevig has served in the Maryland Air National Guard for approximately eighteen years. Her father and brother, both members of the guard, had encouraged her to consider serving in the guard. She recalls her reasons for joining:

Sergeant Deborah Strevig

"I don't think I was committed initially. I didn't understand the guard. I was eighteen years old and quite naive about what the military stood for. I got in for practical reasons. I got out of school in the eleventh grade and I got into the guard to get my **GED** [high school equivalency certificate]."

Because of her lack of skills at the time, Debbie thought that the guard would offer her employment opportunities and a chance to earn extra money.

The possibilities offered by the guard went beyond Debbie's expectations. In addition to educational assistance and retirement benefits, she likes the flexibility of service. Debbie sees the part-time commitment as a way to sample military life without a full-time commitment. She says, "It's a stepping-stone to see if you like this type of deal."

There are opportunities for travel overseas and in the United States. The trips are for relatively short periods of time. For example, guard members may leave their local base for a weekend or for the two-week continuous service period. Members of Debbie's unit have some choice about when and where they travel.

Numerous jobs are available in the guard, and women are allowed to serve in all positions for which they qualify and which are not prohibited by combat exclusion laws or policies. In addition, many jobs provide skill training that may be transferred to the civilian job market.

After working in Operations, Sergeant Strevig moved to Maintenance. Her job title is Weapons System Specialist. She is a weapons load crew chief and frequently supervises the work of men on her crew. She thinks it is difficult for some men to work under the direction of a woman. Weapons loading involves getting planes ready, with bombs or bullets, to fly training missions. Debbie finds her job interesting and says she is still learning new things, even though she has been in the shop for eleven years.

Debbie met her husband, who also serves in the guard, after she joined. They now have two sons. When both parents are in the military, they are required to name a legal guardian for their children (both are under the age of eighteen), in the event that the unit is activated in an emergency. That possibility almost became a reality when there was a chance that the Strevigs' unit would be sent to Saudi Arabia during the Gulf crisis. Under most circumstances Debbie's two sons have reacted well to being a part of a military family, but thoughts of their parents going to Saudi Arabia did worry them. Debbie explained how she and her husband handled the boys' concerns:

"We had to sit down and talk to them. We watched TV together and talked about it. They asked questions and we answered them. If we had gone away, these [questions] wouldn't have been answered. They would have been scared."

While Debbie understands why a lot of people in her guard unit didn't want to go to the Middle East, she was willing to be called. She recalls her reaction when she found out that her unit would not be activated: "All of us that had been here for years were very disappointed that we didn't go. That's what I've trained for all these years and I kinda felt left out."

The Strevigs have not noticed any particular problems associated with being a guard family. Debbie thinks it is probably easier for both husband and wife to be in the guard rather than on active duty. In the guard both are guaranteed assignment in the same area and the unit remains in one place most of the time.

When Debbie joined the guard, she had not anticipated any problems being a woman in a male-dominated environment. She recalls her early experience:

"My concerns came after I enlisted. Back then, in 1974, I was the only female that was connected to Maintenance. It was hard breaking in. It was like opening a door for the rest of the women behind. There were a lot of battles that had to be won and I was chosen. But, in opening the door, after that, it seemed to spread wide open."

In talking about her early experience, Debbie says, "I feel, at that point, I had a lot to prove." Women who served in the Persian Gulf shared similar feelings. Many mentioned that they were viewed as women rather than as soldiers, and many felt they had to do more than men to prove themselves and break the barrier of being female.

Debbie tells of her experience of discrimination after she joined the guard and was in her first assignment area:

"When I got in Operations, any overtime was pushed for the guys. I had to fight to get that. Trips—when you go away on trips—other than the normal two-week active duty—I remember them telling me, 'Oh, there is no way we can take you because there are no quarters set aside for you.' I had to fight for everything which was naturally given to a man. I don't think there is any problem with that now."

Sergeant Strevig thinks attitudes toward women have improved since she first joined the guard.

"They've begun to accept us a lot better. They seem to, you know, the respect is there. We've lost the barriers pretty much in most fields and now I've gotten that done in Maintenance."

Service in the guard has been an interesting and rewarding experience for Sergeant Strevig and she plans to stay in indefinitely. She has encouraged many women, including her sister, to consider the possibility of joining. She offers the following advice to young people who might consider joining the guard:

"It is something to look into . . . something that could really benefit and broaden horizons in a lot of areas. Not only in learning, [but] maybe something that could be added to your civilian job or something you could pursue later. They actually teach you the job and you have a lot of educational benefits. But it's a sense of pride that you can get from being a part [of a family]. It [the guard] has a lot of family things to bring you together. And we try to have a lot of community services. We have fund raisers and stuff. I mean, it has given me back a sense of pride and a sense of, you know, there is a reason for living. There is a reason for being here and I want to be a part of what makes the world go around. So it has given me that."

Debbie feels that the sense of pride and caring extend beyond herself and her own work. She comments about caring for other people and her country when she faced the possibility of going to Saudi Arabia in 1991:

"Even though I had to look at the aspect of leaving my children behind, I also had a sense of pride of being part of keeping my community, my country, free for my children. And that means a lot to me, to be in this unit. This is a good unit and it's come a long way and I'm very proud to be in it."

Compensation and Benefits for Service

The United States Congress determines pay and benefits for the military. Active-duty members of all five branches of the service are paid by the same basic pay scale and receive the same basic benefits. In addition to salary, the military provides other types of compensation, such as housing and food, or pays allowances for them.

Basic pay is the major part of the service person's paycheck. It is determined by rank (also known as pay grade) and length of service. Cost-of-living raises are usually given yearly. In addition to basic pay, military personnel may earn incentives and special pay for certain types of duty. For example, incentives may be earned for hazardous duty, such as flight and submarine duty, parachute jumping, and demolition of explosives. Special pay is offered for sea duty, diving duty, special assignments and service in foreign countries and areas subject to hostile fire. Some branches pay bonuses for choosing certain occupations. The military has special personnel needs for some of the occupations, such as licensed practical nursing and some jobs in the combat arms and intelligence field. A high level of risk associated with the performance of duties in combat arms or intelligence, for example, might also be a reason for a bonus.

Some service members and their families live free of charge in housing on military bases where they are assigned. Those who live off the base receive a housing allowance in addition to basic pay. Food allowances are also provided. The amount of these additional funds varies according to the service member's rank and the number of family members.[8] For example, the full housing allowance for Army officers *without* dependents ranges from $313.20 to $714.90 a month, depending on rank. The range for officers *with* dependents is $425.10 to $879.60. Officers of higher ranks will receive more than those of lower ranks.

Enlisted persons *without* dependents receive between $175.20 and $433.80 a month. The monthly allowance for enlistees *with* dependents ranges from $313.20 to $571.50. These figures represent the basic housing allowance. Adjustments may be made for cost of living in some geographic locations.[9] Since the allowances are not

63

considered part of the basic income, they are not taxed by the federal government. The allowances, combined with the tax savings, represent significant contributions to service members' salaries.

In addition to pay and allowances, military personnel receive other benefits while serving. Full health services (medical and dental) are available to them and most health-care costs for family members are covered. Exchange and commissary privileges offer foods, goods, and services at reduced prices. Military personnel receive thirty days of paid vacation annually and have access to a variety of recreational facilities and entertainment programs. These are offered free of charge or at a very low cost. Educational programs, including tuition assistance at colleges and universities, help some persons earn credits toward or complete undergraduate or graduate degrees. Some free legal services are available to help with personal concerns.

Selected benefits go beyond a person's service obligation. For example, the military offers an excellent retirement program, better than many provided by civilian companies. After twenty years of active-duty service, retirees receive monthly payments of forty percent of their average basic pay for the last five years of active duty. Those who retire after more than twenty years of active duty receive a higher monthly payment. Medical care and commissary and exchange privileges are included in retirement benefits.

Military veterans who complete their service obligation, but do not stay in for at least twenty years until retirement, are also eligible for certain benefits from the Veterans Administration. These might include guarantees for home loans, hospitalization, disability and survivor benefits, educational assistance, and help in finding employment in the civilian labor market.[10]

As you can see, there are many choices and benefits available to people who might consider joining the military. Opportunities and benefits vary somewhat, depending on the branch and type of service chosen (active duty, reserve, or National Guard).

Chapters 5 and 6 describe the options available to enlistees and officers and tells the stories of some women and the choices they made.

CHAPTER
FIVE

Options for Service:
Enlisted and Officer Ranks

There is much to choose from when considering the armed forces as a career. The main choices are the branch of service and either a full- or part-time service obligation. Another important consideration is whether to join the enlisted or officer ranks. There are several differences between these two options, including qualifications, training programs, types of jobs, level of responsibility, and pay.

In this chapter you'll read about the enlisted and officer ranks and meet women who serve in both areas. Their personal stories might help you make a decision about which option to choose if you are considering joining the military. It is important to note that the chapter describes the situation for enlisted women who serve on active duty, that is, on a full-time basis. There will be some differences for those who choose to join the reserves or the National Guard. Local recruiters have more information about the differences.

Unless otherwise indicated, the factual information in this chapter is taken from *Military Careers: A Guide to Military Occupations and Selected Military Career Paths, 1992–1994* published by the Department of Defense.[1] The guide, which provides detailed information about job specialties in the officer and enlisted ranks, can be found at all recruitment offices.

Enlisted Members—The "Backbone"

Enlisted members are the "backbone" of the armed forces. They carry out the daily work of the military. They are similar to employees in civilian companies who perform trade, craft, clerical, and technical jobs. Some enlisted members with more experience and higher ranks supervise enlistees with less experience and lower ranks.

The military offers a wide variety of job choices to enlistees. While opportunities vary somewhat by service, in combination, the five branches (Air Force, Army, Navy, Marines, and Coast Guard) offer training and employment in over two thousand enlisted job specialties. The specialties are organized into twelve broad groups: Human Services; Media and Public Affairs; Health Care; Engineering, Science, and Technical; Administrative; Service; Vehicle and Machinery Mechanic; Electronic and Electrical Equipment Repair; Construction; Machine Operator and Precision Work; Transportation and Material Handling; and Combat Specialty. As noted in previous chapters, women are kept out of some specialty areas in each branch because of combat exclusion laws or policies.

Since many military jobs correspond to jobs in the civilian workforce, people who leave the military after completing their service obligation may find it easier to locate civilian jobs than those who have not had the specialized training.

Qualifications for Enlistees

The general qualification categories for enlistees include age, citizenship status, physical condition, education, aptitude (determined by entry test scores), moral character, and marital status and dependents (see Table 1 on page 131). It is important to remember that each service has specific enlistment requirements. Again this information is available from local recruiters for the specific branches.

The first step in enlisting in the military involves talking with a recruiter. The addresses and phone numbers for recruiters in your area are probably listed in your local telephone directory. Sometimes recruiters visit high schools or set up information booths at community gatherings, such as job fairs or athletic events. Recruiters provide detailed information about the qualifications and opportunities in their service and start the enlistment process.

Enlisted women practice firing an M-60 during Marine Corps basic training.

Training and Education

The United States military usually offers four types of training to enlisted members. After **induction** the new enlistee attends basic training, sometimes called recruit training or "basic" or boot camp. This includes orientation to military life and instruction in military skills and physical conditioning (also called fitness training). The length and specific content of the initial training varies by service. The length of basic training is six weeks for the Air Force, eight weeks for the Army, eight weeks and three days for the Navy, eleven weeks for male marines and twelve weeks for female marines.

67

Enlisted women in the Marine Corps train for a week longer than men for several reasons. The women train in smaller groups and receive more weapons training during this phase because they do not have the extended combat-skills training taken by men after "basic" and before job-specialty training. The Marine Corps women go straight to job training after they complete the basic program.[2]

After completing basic training, **recruits** usually enter job training to learn the skills they will need to work in their job specialties. Many jobs are open to women. Some of these jobs are in health care, mechanics, transport, electronics, air traffic control, public affairs, data analysis, and intelligence. Instruction is offered in the classroom and on the job, with the length of the program varying according to the specialty. The more complicated the job, the longer the program.

Advanced training courses are available to enlistees throughout their military careers. The courses help improve technical skills and also teach about supervisory and management responsibilities. Individual courses and special schools offer leadership training to enlistees who supervise other military personnel.

Once in the military, enlistees have many opportunities to continue their education. They may enroll in courses to advance their job skills or to learn in areas of general interest, such as art, music, literature, history, or psychology. In fact, some enlistees take enough courses to earn a college degree. In 1987, for example, 19,277 military personnel earned associate degrees, 6,037 earned bachelor's degrees, and 7,019 earned graduate degrees.[3]

After completing job training, enlistees are assigned to a **duty station.** All the military services require their members to change duty locations at specified intervals. The usual assignment to a specific location, referred to as a "tour of duty," or a "tour," is from three to four years, but there are exceptions. The United States military has bases in most states and in numerous foreign countries. For example, a service member might be assigned to a tour in Germany, Italy, Turkey, Norway, Spain, the United Kingdom, Australia, the Republic of Korea, Thailand, Bahrain, Egypt, or Saudi Arabia. Navy ships also dock in the ports of many foreign countries. Assignment to one of these bases or ships allows travel to many cities and countries all over the world. Many enlisted members, particularly the single enlistees, believe that the frequent foreign travel is a major benefit of military service.

68

Pay Grades and Ranks

There are nine enlisted **pay grades,** which correspond to ranks, in each service. They range from E-1 to E-9, with E-1 being the lowest. Salary is determined by pay grade and length of service. New recruits begin at the lowest pay grade and rank (E-1), unless the specific service allows a person to enter at a higher grade because he or she has technical job skills that are needed by the military. For example, Army enlistees who have experience or advanced training as machinists, information-systems operators, or photo and layout specialists would enter at a higher pay grade.[4] Promotion within the lower pay grades is fairly routine for enlistees whose progress and job performance are satisfactory. Promotion to E-4 and higher pay grades requires superior performance and is more competitive. Length of time in the service and in the present pay grade also influence advancement in the enlisted ranks. (See Table 2 on page 132 for pay grades and ranks for enlisted members.)

A summary of general employment benefits for enlisted members is given in Table 3 on page 133. Specific information about each of the services is available from recruiters.

Sergeant First Class Earnestine Richardson

In the following section, Sergeant First Class Earnestine Richardson describes her experiences as an enlisted woman in the Army. While the experiences of enlisted women vary greatly, Sergeant Richardson's comments provide an interesting and personal example.

Sergeant First Class Earnestine Richardson has served in the military for seventeen years. After graduation from high school, she worked as a data transcriber for a civilian company. When she joined the Army in 1974, she was twenty-two years old, married, and had two young children. She thought the military offered educational and medical benefits as well as opportunities for travel.

Sergeant Richardson and her sister joined the Army at the same time. When asked why she chose the Army, rather than one of the other services, she responded: "The opportunities made available to me were greater in the Army. I thought opportunities in the Army for women were endless." She said that limitations placed on women by combat exclusion laws and policies were not an issue for her,

"Because I had no interest in the areas closed to women, I was not concerned."

She entered at the rank of private (E-1) and took basic training at Fort Jackson, South Carolina. When she entered, men and women trained at the same location, but in separate groups. She remembers the academic course work in the classroom as being easier than the physical training. She thinks the bonds that formed between women who shared the experience made adjustment easier for them.

"The women in my company formed many support networks to assist each other. If someone could press their uniform better than someone who could spit-shine their boots, they swapped. The one who could iron best ironed the uniforms, and the one who could shine the boots best shined the boots. These swaps took place in many areas. Someone more knowledgeable of the skills required would take time in the evening to go over them, to explain them so even the slowest person could understand. There was always a sense of camaraderie."

Sergeant Richardson enjoys the variety of job experiences the military provides.

"I joined the Army as a military policewoman. I'd always wanted to be a policewoman, but didn't have the educational background to pursue it on the outside. I've attended the Defense Equal Opportunity Management Institute. I've trained as an Executive Administrative Assistant and I'm currently working in the **protocol** field. Additionally, I manage the Distinguished Visitors' Quarters."

After serving a year and a half, Sergeant Richardson met her current husband, who was also in the Army military police corps. She commented on some couples' concerns about both husband and wife being members of the military:

"For me it has been easy being married to a military person. For one reason, we've both been assured of being employed, regardless of where we were sent. The difficulties could be not being assigned in the same area as your husband or wife, although I did not have that problem."

There are some potential problems as well as benefits for children in military families in Sergeant Richardson's view.

"Having to be mobile, I'm sure is a great problem for the children. Always having to leave friends behind and move on can be a problem *and* a benefit. Their growth level exceeds that of children in the civilian environment because of their adaptive skills and worldly experiences."

The differences in the treatment of men and women were greater in Sergeant Richardson's early years of service than they are today.

"They [women] were expected to make coffee only because they were women and to set up social functions because of the attitude that these were women's things as opposed to men's things."

Things *have* changed since Sergeant Richardson first enlisted: "I think the situation for military women has changed somewhat because of the change in attitudes toward women. I feel women are accepted better and the job opportunities have increased, as well as the confidence level." Even though some inequalities still exist because of limitations set by combat exclusion laws and policies, she thinks the opportunities are greater for military women than for those in civilian jobs.

Sergeant Richardson plans to stay in the Army for at least two more years, when she will be eligible for retirement. She thinks the variety of experiences that the military has offered will provide a sound background for success in the civilian world. Looking back at her military career, she offered this assessment:

"Overall, I evaluate my experience in the military as a very positive one. It has provided me with the environment and experiences to enhance my growth, maturity and knowledge, as well as understanding of other people." When asked if she would choose to enlist, knowing what she now knows, she responded, "Definitely, it's my open door."

She offers the following suggestion to people who might be thinking about joining the military:

71

"I would advise anyone who is considering the military as an *occupation* to know what they want, examine their motives, make a definite choice and go for it. The military has a lot to offer in the positive and it would truly be an experience of a lifetime, one that I would choose all over again. . . ."

Sergeant Richardson is enthusiastic about the future for military women.

"I believe the future holds numerous opportunities for women in the military. I see the future as exciting and positive, offering diverse choices. I perceive many doors of opportunity opening and women seizing them as they are made available."

In the remaining pages of this chapter you will be given some general information about officers who serve full time in the active-duty military. Then you will read about the personal experience of a woman officer in the Air Force. Recruiters will be able to provide details about the differences found for officers who serve in the reserves or the National Guard.

Officers—Professional Leaders

Officers are the professional leaders in the military. Their responsibilities are similar to those of corporate managers or executives in the civilian workplace. They lead and command other officers and enlisted members in carrying out military activities. As leaders they serve as models of behavior for others as they reinforce the values and goals of the military. When they command they direct others and are in charge of their activities. In contrast to enlisted members, officers' responsibilities are broad, going beyond the duties of their specific occupational fields. They are responsible for the performance and well being of all personnel under their supervision.

Military officers may choose from a wide variety of managerial, professional, and scientific occupations. For example, some provide medical care and legal services to service members and their families. There are a number of jobs in science, engineering, and related fields. Officers may also serve as pilots and as leaders in specialty areas, including elite **special operations** such as Navy

SEALS, Army Rangers, and Green Berets. They also serve in the infantry, armor (tank and other armored vehicles), missiles, artillery, intelligence, and naval operations.

There are more than fifteen hundred job specialties for officers in the five services combined. The specialties are grouped into nine broad areas: Executive, Administrative, and Managerial; Human Services; Media and Public Affairs; Health Diagnosing and Treating Practitioner; Health Care; Engineering, Science, and Technical; Service; Transportation; and Combat Specialty.

The availability of particular job specialties varies somewhat by service, depending on its mission. Female officers have fewer choices than males because of combat exclusion laws and policies. For example, women officers cannot choose jobs in the special operations mentioned here. Opportunities for women, however, continue to expand.

Qualifications for Officers

The general categories of qualifications for officers are similar to those for enlisted members, but specific requirements differ for some categories. (See Table 4 on page 134.) Specific requirements also differ from one branch of the service to another. Detailed information is available from recruiters.

There are four avenues to becoming a commissioned officer in today's military: Reserve Officer's Training Corps (ROTC), **Officer Candidate School/Officer Training School (OCS/OTS)**, the **service academies**, and **direct appointment.** These options are discussed in detail in Chapter 6. When a person successfully completes one of these programs, he or she is **commissioned**. Commissioning is a type of certification that assigns the officer rank, authority, and obligation.

Training and Education

Officer's training and education last throughout the officer's career. While each branch of the service offers specific programs for officer development, all branches share some general similarities. Officers are offered five types of training and educational opportunities: basic officer training, job training, advanced training, professional military education, and leadership training.

Midshipmen at the United States Naval Academy train to become officers.

During basic officer training, the candidates receive all the material necessary for becoming a military officer. For example, an officer candidate learns about the responsibilities of military officers, military traditions, customs, laws and regulations, military science, leadership, career development, and administrative procedures; in other words, everything a person needs to know to lead. Physical conditioning is also a part of most programs.

The length and timing of basic officer training may differ, depending on the way one chooses to become an officer and on the branch of service. For example, there are differences between programs provided by ROTC, OCS/OTS, and the service academies. In ROTC the training is spread out over a longer period of time because ROTC **cadets** are also college students and military training is taken on a part-time basis. People who enter the OCS program train for ten weeks in the Marines, fourteen weeks in the Army, and those in the Navy receive sixteen weeks of training. The OTS program in the Air Force lasts for fifteen weeks.[5] The content of training is spread out over the four-year course of study at the service academies.

Job training follows basic training. The length of initial job training varies according to the specialty. Officer job training extends beyond the initial training period because officers are leaders and need to learn about the broad areas under their command. Since they are responsible for the performance and well-being of personnel in their unit, officers continue to learn about the jobs that they supervise but don't actually perform. In addition to technical training, officers take part in programs that are related to their positions of responsibility. For example, they may take courses in military history and strategy and leadership and management skills.

There are two categories of advanced training for officers. One includes courses that provide information about the technical skills that will be used in future assignments. The other category instructs officers about the general mission of their particular job and how to coordinate the different operations associated with the job's mission.

Courses in professional military education prepare officers for future responsibilites in leadership, management, and other areas associated with advanced rank. Officers receive leadership training, formal and informal, throughout their careers.

Continuing education is also an important part of an officer's career development. It can have a major influence on that person's career advancement. The United States military offers several continuing education programs. Some lead to advanced degrees and others offer broad knowledge in areas of interest to the military and the officer. These might include courses in sociology, psychology, history, international relations, political science, and management.

After job training, officers are assigned to a duty station, usually for a period of from three to four years. Duty assignments are usually determined by the needs of the service and officers' career needs for broad experience. Officers' preferences are considered whenever possible. Some duty stations are more attractive than others. During the Cold War, for example, many duty stations were located in western Europe. Military personnel liked these assignments because of the comfortable physical environment and the opportunities for travel to beautiful and interesting places. With the collapse of communism and the end of Cold War tensions, the number of duty assignments in western Europe has been reduced. However, as regional tensions develop in southeastern Europe and the former Soviet Union, United States military personnel might be sent to these areas previously closed to them. These duty stations, along with those in other parts of the world, present specific challenges.

Pay Grades and Ranks for Officers

Pay grade and length of service determine an officer's pay. There are ten officer pay grades, ranging from 0-1 to 0-10, with 0-1 being the lowest. Each pay grade corresponds to a rank. (See Table 5 on page 135.) Newly commissioned officers usually enter at the 0-1 level. Persons with professional credentials, such as doctors, nurses, and lawyers, who enter through direct appointment, may enter at higher grades. Direct appointment is discussed in Chapter 6.

Administrative boards usually make decisions about the promotion of officers in the lower pay grades (0-1 and 0-2). Advancement is based on satisfactory performance, recommendation of commander, and spending a specific period of time in the pay grade. While these early promotions are fairly routine, advancement to E-4 and the higher ranks requires more superior qualifications and is more competitive because the number of available slots is limited by Congress. Selection boards, consisting of senior officers, make recommendations for advancement to the higher officer ranks. Opportunities for advancement may change in the 1990s as the military reduces the size of the force.

General information about pay, allowances, and benefits was presented in Chapter 4. A summary of employment benefits for officers can be found in Table 6 on page 136. More detailed information is available from recruiters.

In the following pages, you'll meet a young woman who graduated from college, worked, and traveled before deciding to become an Air Force officer.

Captain Kathryn Lindsay Townsend

Kathryn Lindsay Townsend graduated from college in 1982 with a bachelor's degree in business administration. Her college years were demanding because of course work and participation on the women's lacrosse team. Away from school, Lindsay was busy with part-time work as a waitress and family responsibilities that included helping care for her elderly grandmother.

Lindsay recalls the time after graduation and the factors that influenced her to consider joining the military. Advertisements, mainly on radio and TV, rather than personal contacts, brought the possibility to her attention. Her uncle and father had served in the military in World War II, but military service was not an established family tradition. A trip she took after college graduation seemed to influence her choice of the military rather than a civilian job.

"Right after college I took a trip around the world for a year. When I returned, I worked as a waitress temporarily, just to regroup after being away for so long. And I looked into the opportunity of getting into the Air Force.

When I was traveling around the world, I developed a tremendous interest in living overseas. To actually live in another country and be productive is very difficult. I thought by going in the military I would have that opportunity. That was the driving force. Secondly, my degree is in business administration and I really didn't have the desire to be either a secretary or an office manager or to go into sales. That is what I felt would initially be open to me with just an undergraduate degree. So I looked into the Air Force for those reasons: to have the opportunity to live overseas, to have an income, to be able to live on my own."

Lindsay talked to recruiters and considered the possibilities in each of the services before choosing the Air Force. She explained her choice:

"I picked the Air Force because I believed that the opportunities were greater for women than in the Army or Navy. I felt that the Army and Navy had a tradition that was a lot more male-dominated

Captain Kathryn Lindsay Townsend

and more male-oriented. The job functions were more geared toward males. The Air Force was more technology oriented. I suspected that the Air Force would have more opportunities for women. I also thought that, since it was more high tech, there would be a higher quality of individuals in terms of educational background. So I thought it would be the best for me.''

Lindsay was not especially concerned about the general acceptance of women in the military. Nor was she concerned about her own acceptance in a male-dominated environment.

''I think that because of my athletic background and my participation in sports and having to interact with males in their world, I've grown up very comfortable with that [being a woman in a male environment]. I thought I would be able to make those adjustments. For every female, I don't know if that would be the case.''

Since Lindsay had a college degree, she could choose between joining the enlisted or officer ranks. She explained why she chose to become an officer:

"The biggest difference is leadership. When you start out in the enlisted ranks, you're going to be a 'worker bee.' You're going to be at a lower level. With a college degree, I think I would have been a little frustrated doing something at a lower level and having someone telling me what to do. The pay is better for officers and that's part of it, too. If you want to go enlisted, that's great because it's a tremendous life, a good life. But it's quite a different world between being enlisted and an officer."

Lindsay was twenty-six years old when she reported to Officer's Training School at Lackland Air Force Base in Texas. When she entered, women attended basic officer's training with men. Lindsay remembers some of the experiences from this training period and the different requirements for men and women:

"The physical test was different. I can't remember exactly but it wasn't as difficult for the women as it was for the men. We had both male and female instructors. I personally was instructed only by males, but there were female instructors there."

A common feeling among military women is the need to prove themselves in the male-dominated environment. Lindsay shared her feelings about this concern:

"I felt the need to do that. Not so much that I felt pressure coming from them [men], but an internal pressure I placed on myself. When I was in Officer's Training School, there was a position called Lower Flight Captain that is selected by commissioned officers in the school. I was one of the few females that was selected to do this. I was in charge of all the new officer trainees coming in. I had about twenty people under me and I wrote their reports and I evaluated them. I think if there were any reservations about picking a female, he [the flight commander] wouldn't have done so because how I did was also a reflection on the flight commander who selected me.

As a female, I was probably more critical of my female counterparts than males were simply because I always wanted them [the females] to be able to do well. Because I had an athletic background, I always did well on the physical training tests and I felt they should be able to keep up standards too. But I think you realize that that's only one aspect of leadership and that it's not all that important an aspect. As long as they can meet the minimum standard and they didn't bring the team down, they [women] were viewed as positive members of the team. I don't remember a lot of griping. I think there is such a need to pull together in OTS that you don't tend to do that."

Lindsay believes that this need resulted in an emphasis on the shared experiences of officer trainees and the need to work together, rather than focusing on the differences between men and women.

The needs of the service are considered first when assigning new officers to a specialty area, but they are allowed to state their choices in order of preference. After she completed basic officer training, Lindsay began specialty training in the intelligence field, which was her first choice. Her past experiences in studying political science and traveling around the world influenced her interest in this area.

"The intelligence career field is one in which you analyze what's happening around the world. I felt that it would be an area that would hold my interest and it's something I could contribute."

Military women have reported various incidents, some obvious and some more subtle, of sexual discrimination and sexual harassment. When asked if she had problems in either area, Lindsay described her experiences:

"If I have, it has been very subtle. I wouldn't have any concrete example where I sat down and said, 'They didn't send me to that because I'm a woman.' I probably had experienced it maybe through other people. Maybe they made comments and things like that. There definitely are men in the Air Force who don't believe women should be there. They don't voice that opinion because Air Force policy [is] clearly against that kind of comment."

At one point in her career, Lindsay was to be assigned to a new unit—one that had not previously included women. The Air Force delayed her application until the commander retired. They knew he would not select a woman to join the unit, even if she were qualified. The new commander agreed to take a woman and Lindsay was a kind of pioneer when she joined the all-male unit.

"I remember one person saying, 'Do you realize that you are the first woman to be in this unit?' He kept saying that and it was a little unnerving at first, but I settled in. Actually, now that you've asked me, I remember that I was treated completely different by the duty officer. This other guy and I arrived on the same day. He was told to go up to the Pentagon and **in-process**. I was driven to the Pentagon by another officer, escorted through the whole in-processing, and driven back. The guy was given his identification and was out doing his job probably within two weeks. My duty officer was like, 'Let's see how you do' because I was the first woman. So, yes, now that I think of it, I was really handled differently. I guess I tried to forget that. Looking back, I think the duty officer regretted it because he said, 'I just wasn't sure how you were going to handle certain things and I just wanted to be a little bit more careful because the job is sensitive and important.' I believe that he didn't have very much faith in women being able to do the work and so he didn't want to put me in a position . . . if he felt I wasn't going to be able to handle it. The same unit is now more than fifty percent female."

Lindsay admits that she has personally experienced sexual harassment and knows of other women who have also. She believes the Air Force is concerned about this type of behavior and has taken steps to prevent it.

"They [the Air Force] take it very seriously. I wouldn't say it is prevalent, I'd say it's there. I think it's changing as you become exposed to commanders who are of the younger generation. Their socialization process is different. They're much more aware of how you should treat women. It's the older generation that has gotten away with it for years."

She believes that women's participation in the Persian Gulf War helped to change attitudes toward military women.

"I think Desert Storm [the name given by the military to the Persian Gulf War] proved that women can handle the pressures. I'm sure there are instances where maybe a guy hesitated or did something he wouldn't have done because a woman was there. But for the most part, I heard stories where guys said, 'Well, I'd rather have a woman who knows what she's doing than some guy who doesn't have a clue and I have to trust in that person.' A lot of military interaction involves trust."

In addition to more specific complaints about sexual discrimination and sexual harassment, Lindsay commented on general aspects of military service that may be viewed as negative by some members:

"You do have to get up and move quite often—every three years. Right now, as a single person, that's not a problem. But [it might be] if I were married or if I had to be separated from my family. On the flip side of that it's dynamic. You're going to meet interesting people every time you move and the Air Force family is very strong. You can go to any Air Force base and feel like you belong. It's very comfortable."

She also mentioned how the attitudes of people in society at large might have a negative effect on service members' experiences:

"There are lots of times when a lot of people view the military negatively. If you're a part of that, you're going to get the kind of prejudice and discrimination that goes with it. Most of that is ignorance on a person's part. They don't understand what the military is about. The problems, the things I dislike about the military, I believe exist in the outside world. I think the kinds of things that frustrate me about the military are things that I would be frustrated with in general. I think it's a very good life!"

The Air Force has provided Captain Townsend with many opportunities and she is quite satisfied with her experiences. She mentioned many that she might not have had if she hadn't joined.

"I think the Air Force teaches you things that you don't necessarily get in college. One is . . . how to communicate in written form. How to speak in public [is another]. It teaches you how to deal with prejudice. You can't be prejudiced in the military. You're going to work next to a black person, an Asian person. You're going to do it and get along. You may not like it because your socialization may make you a bigot, but you're going to learn how to deal with people."

Captain Townsend noted how military service can help develop personal growth and interpersonal skills:

"You're going to learn how to be financially responsible or you get kicked out. You're not going to get messed up on drugs and if you do, you're going to get kicked out. The military is a system that deals with accountabilities. You're held accountable for what you do or don't do. And you are rewarded on merit. If you do well, you're going to get rewarded, and if you don't do well there are consequences."

Air Force experiences may contribute to personal growth in other ways, as Lindsay points out:

"It gives you time to mature, to be on your own and travel. I water-skied in the Panama Canal and had lunch in Honduras. I've been to Egypt and Korea. I've had all these experiences that I would never have had in any other kind of job. It's just a great way to have some fun. . . . I think it's a great way to start."

In addition to interpersonal skills and personal responsibility and growth, Lindsay mentioned that there are many opportunities to develop technical skills that might be useful in civilian jobs when a person leaves the military.

Lindsay has been promoted to the rank of Captain (0-3) and plans to stay in the Air Force as long as it fits with her personal situation. Based on what she knows now, she would make the decision to join the military. She points out the one thing that she might do differently:

"I think if I had it to do all over again, I would choose ROTC. My college educational experience was limited at times because of family obligations. I think if I had been in an ROTC program I would have had a free ride financially, and I would have had the ROTC socialization and camaraderie."

Captain Townsend admits that her initial reasons for joining were practical. She describes the change in her motivations for serving:

"Having been in the military and experiencing that world, I've become very patriotic. I love when the national anthem is played and I have a lot of pride when I stand in my uniform. I'm in a world that's unique. You don't feel that when you first come in. It is fostered by being in the military."

She offers the following advice to people who might consider joining:

"If you really don't know what you want to do and you want an opportunity to experience living on your own, in a way that's going to be productive, if you want to get training and have a sense of belonging, the military is a great place to start. It's not for everyone. It's not to go into the military to be an officer for twenty or thirty years. Very few people go into the military thinking that. But . . . go in and have a chance to grow up a little and have some rare opportunities."

This chapter has offered a general overview of some differences between the enlisted and officer ranks. As you can tell, the women interviewed see the military as a place to be somebody, to develop and learn and test themselves, to be part of a family, and to make a contribution to their country.

Chapter 6 provides information about the different avenues to becoming a commissioned officer and tells some of the personal experiences of two female midshipmen at the United States Naval Academy.

CHAPTER
SIX

Becoming an Officer:
How You Get There

Being an officer means being a leader. If this is your choice, how do you become a military officer? Each of the options described in Chapter 5 is discussed in detail in the following pages. You'll also read about the experiences of two female students at the Naval Academy, the main training ground for career officers in the United States Navy.

Reserve Officers' Training Corps (ROTC)

College students may receive training to become officers in the Air Force, Army, Navy, or Marines by joining a Reserve Officers' Training Corps program, commonly called ROTC. The programs are offered in more than fourteen hundred public and private colleges and universities throughout the United States. If you attend a school that does not offer ROTC, it is often possible to join a unit at a school located in the same vicinity. ROTC is the largest supplier of officers to the United States military. About forty-four percent of the new officers who enter the armed forces each year have chosen this route of entry. ROTC is *not* available for the Coast Guard.

Students who join ROTC are called cadets. In addition to meeting the college or university requirements, they take part in military-related activities. The ROTC curriculum combines courses in military science with training exercises to prepare officers for active duty, the reserves, and the National Guard (Air Force and Army). Courses are taught in organization and management, national defense, military history, military tactics, and leadership. Cadets generally take part in drills for several hours each week and in more demanding training exercises for a few weeks during the summer. The requirements and length of training (from two to four years) vary by service and the type of ROTC plan selected.

Uniforms and supplies required for military courses are provided by the service. In addition, cadets who attend the advanced course during their junior and senior years in college may receive an allowance of approximately $100 a month. ROTC programs offer some scholarships that cover tuition, educational fees, books, supplies, uniforms, and a yearly allowance of approximately $1,000. Not all people who apply for a scholarship will receive one, however. An applicant must compete with others on a national basis.

After graduation from college, ROTC candidates become commissioned officers and have to meet a service obligation. The usual obligation is eight years, with the time being divided between active duty and the reserves or the National Guard. The needs of the particular service determine how the time is divided.[1]

More detailed information about ROTC programs may be obtained from local recruiters.

Officer Candidate School and Officer Training School (OCS/OTS)

Programs for college graduates *without* military experience are called Officer Candidate School (OCS) by the Army, Navy, and Marines and Officer Training School (OTS) by the Air Force. Captain Lindsay Townsend, whose story was presented in Chapter 5, graduated from OTS.

People interested in this path of entry apply at a local recruiting office during their senior year in college. College graduates under twenty-nine years of age may also apply. Candidates enter the OCS/OTS program as enlisted members.

The length of OCS/OTS varies from ten to eighteen weeks, depending on the branch of service. Upon successful completion of the program, graduates become commissioned officers. The service obligation ranges from three to eight years, depending on the branch of service and job specialty. For example, Army officers are required to serve a minimum of three years on active duty. Jet pilots in the Air

Force, Navy, and Marines have a minimum obligation of eight years of active duty. Approximately twenty-one percent of the new military officers who join the armed forces each year enter through this route.[2]

Direct Appointment

Qualified professionals, such as doctors, nurses, lawyers, engineers, priests, ministers, and rabbis, are eligible for direct appointment as military officers. They receive a minimum of military training and must serve for at least two years. Civil engineers who enter the Navy through direct appointment must serve a minimum of four years. Upon graduation, college students preparing to enter these fields may apply for scholarships in return for a longer service obligation after they complete their professional training. Each year approximately eleven percent of the new military officers enter the services through direct appointment.[3]

The Service Academies

The purpose of the service academies is to prepare young men and women, morally, mentally, and physically, to become professional officers in the United States armed forces. Many of the graduates become career officers. Four service academies provide education and training to men and women who will become commissioned officers in one of the branches of the United States military. They include the United States Air Force Academy (**USAFA**) in Colorado Springs, Colorado; the United States Military Academy (**USMA**—Army) in West Point, New York; the United States Naval Academy (**USNA**—Navy and Marines) in Annapolis, Maryland; and the United States Coast Guard Academy (**USCGA**) in New London, Connecticut. Approximately thirteen percent of the military officers who enter the armed forces each year are academy graduates.[4]

Women were admitted to the Coast Guard Academy in 1975, and first entered the other academies in 1976. Women make up about seventeen percent of the class of 1994 at the Coast Guard Academy. The figures are slightly lower for the other academies, where women make up around eleven percent of those entering in a class.[5] Figures reported by *USA Today* (June 2, 1992) showed that the percentage of

The United States Naval Academy started to admit women in 1976.

women who actually graduate ranges from 9.3 at the Naval Academy to 14.1 at the Coast Guard Academy. The percentages for the Air Force Academy and West Point were 11.9 and 11.3, respectively. Because of some limitations on female officers' assignments, the number of women who attend the military academies is limited, compared to women's attendance in civilian universities, where they receive 54 percent of the bachelor's degrees annually.

The requirements for appointment to all the academies are as follows:

Age: at least seventeen years of age, but not past twenty-second birthday by July 1 of the year of entry
Citizenship: United States citizen (international students, citizens of other countries, who are invited by the United States government are exempt from this requirement)
Marital Status: unmarried, not pregnant, no legal obligations for support of another individual
Character: high moral character
Other: meet academic, physical, and medical standards

Applicants to the USAFA, USNA, and West Point must also obtain a nomination. This is not required by the Coast Guard Academy.

How does a student go about getting a nomination? Nominations are usually obtained from members of Congress, such as the United States representative from your congressional district or one of your United States senators. Other sources include the president and vice-president of the United States and several categories of military-related nominations. Enlisted personnel in the active duty and reserve forces and children of deceased or disabled veterans, of prisoners of war, of servicemen missing in action, or of Medal of Honor winners may request a military-related nomination. The Secretary of each of the specific branches of service is another source in this category. It is not necessary to know the nominee personally.

Details about specific sources and the way to solicit nominations may be obtained from the guidance office at the academy of your choice. It is important to remember that admission to the academies requires a lot of paper work. High school students interested in applying to one or more of the service academies should begin the process early in their junior year.[6]

Admission to the academies is extremely competitive. For example, about twelve thousand students applied for entrance to the graduating class of 1994 at the Naval Academy. Approximately fifteen hundred were offered admission and about twelve hundred accepted. Approximately eleven percent of those admitted were women.[7] For those who are admitted, the service academies provide many benefits. Students receive a full scholarship with paid tuition, room and board, free medical and dental care, and a monthly salary

A Navy midshipman training to become a pilot. As of 1993, women in the Navy have a chance to fly fighter planes in any situation, not just for training and testing.

or allowance of approximately $540. The allowance is used for uniforms, books, supplies, and personal expenses.

New classes enter at the end of June or in early July of each year. The four-year program provides students with a broad education. The academic curriculum, which leads to a bachelor's degree, includes courses in a variety of subjects. The available majors will differ according to the service academy. Several major courses of study are offered at each. These include majors in basic sciences, social sciences, humanities, and engineering. Some of the majors are specific to the mission of the particular branch of service. For example, **midshipmen** at the Naval Academy may major in marine engineering, ocean engineering, naval architecture, or oceanography. Cadets at the Air Force Academy can choose majors in aeronautics and astronautics.

Professional training consists of courses and training related to leadership and the military activities of the particular branch of service. Participation in physical education and athletics, either intercollegiate or intramural, is required. Numerous professional, recreational, and athletic extracurricular activities are available at each of the academies. Graduates become commissioned officers and are required to complete an active-duty service obligation of at least five years.[8]

Detailed information about the programs and service obligations can be obtained by contacting the academies directly.

Women at The United States Naval Academy: Some Personal Experiences

The service academies offer young men and women exciting opportunities to learn, to grow, to lead, and to serve their country. In the remaining pages of this chapter, two female midshipmen share some of their experiences as students at the United States Naval Academy.

Andrea Louise Lemon

Andrea Louise Lemon, a senior at the Naval Academy, was interviewed a short time before her graduation in May 1991. Here she tells about her family background, her interest in the military, and her experiences as a midshipman:

"I had a very unusual upbringing. Both of my grandfathers were in the Army. One was an officer and one was enlisted. Both my uncles on my mother's side were enlisted in the Navy. My father's brother was in the Army. He was an officer. My dad was a naval officer and from the day I was born, I was moving all over the world. It was a lot of fun and we had lots of friends. But, when you get to be about the age of seven, it really gets hard to leave your friends. Then, after the first time you move, you realize that you'll always make new friends

Midshipman Andrea Louise Lemon

wherever you go and you'll keep your old friends and go back and see them and they'll always remember who you were. What's very positive is that you get a very broad experience."

Several factors combined to determine Andrea's choice of the Naval Academy:

"My dad was in the Navy. I like the water. That is probably what it really was. From the age of three, I was sailing. There was one woman [officer]. She was a civil engineer [and] a Naval Academy graduate. She was also a sailor, and I'm a sailor. I wanted to come here before I talked to her, but that clinched it.

I decided to come to the Naval Academy because I thought if you wanted to be the best at what you were doing, you should come to the place that makes the best. And so, having read all the catalogs of

92

the Naval Academy, having talked to a few grads, I said, 'This has to be the best place. It's full-time military experience.' I just thought the Navy was the best place for someone who really loved the water."

Some future midshipmen find the academy's application procedure quite tedious. Andrea commented on the process when she applied:

"I wrote letters to all my senators. They send you back a letter saying that you have an interview with one of their people and they decide whether they will give you a nomination. I got President Bush's nomination when he was vice-president. You have to have a family member in the military to get a vice-presidential nomination. I also got one from a senator [who was] on the Armed Forces Committee at the time.

You have to send a lot of forms back to the Naval Academy. You have to have a physical test and get recommendations from several people. Then you go to the local naval hospital and take all these medical tests. You have to be persistent because not all the paper work is going to go through correctly. I think that's what really helps in getting in—persistence."

Andrea commented on her concerns about being a woman in a male-dominated environment and describes some of her early experiences at the academy:

"Women had been here for about ten years [since 1976]. A woman who graduated from the academy, Sandy, [told me about] what to expect. At first, be yourself. Some women are too feminine. They get offended if a guy says something that is slightly rude. You just have to get used to the fact that they're not doing this on purpose, it's just the way they are. Most guys are really nice here. They treat you like their sister. You heard things at first, like that some of the guys might try to run you out because you're female. That is true, actually. When I was coming in, there was one guy, just one, who wanted to run women out. That was his mission. But, if you stick together. . . . that's what they teach you—teamwork—you're not going to have problems with that.

I didn't have any fears about coming in, except the day after we were sworn in. The first day you get here they're pretty nice to you. Then, after you're sworn in, that's when all the yelling starts. I guess at first they want to scare you. That kind of scared me, but you have roommates . . . that's when you stick together. When you're in a group, there's no problem with fear at all. I think it's good when you go in a group. If you were the only woman, it would be different."

Women do stand out at the academy. Andrea recalled the one situation in which she was the only female:

"I was the only girl in one class, one time. You sort of feel awkward at first. First the class starts getting a lab partner. Of course, all the guys are buddy-buddy and they all hook up. But the guys really don't mind having a girl for a partner. It works out real well."

She believes that past experiences influence some of the male midshipmen's attitudes toward their female classmates.

"Some of them [the guys] don't know how to deal with women. We had one guy in our company [who] didn't know how to deal with women. Just about every female slammed him. The company officer went and had a talk with him and the next semester, he was the nicest guy. Sometimes even the group will recognize that one of their classmates is having problems and they'll say, 'Look, you better straighten out how you handle such and such a person.'"

There are groups at the academy that provide a support network for women. Lectures and other activities related to women's interests are offered and men are always welcome to attend the women's activities.

Women resign from the academy for a number of reasons. Some are personal and others might be similar to those of men who leave. Women also leave for the same reasons that some people give for leaving a civilian college. Andrea offered her thoughts about why women might choose to resign from the academy:

"I think most of the women who leave realized the Navy just wasn't for them. They thought, 'I'd rather go home and have a family.' They weren't as well informed, as perhaps they should have been about what their commitment was really like. Other women left because of grades. They just couldn't handle it."

Andrea compared the academic standards for midshipmen with those of students in civilian institutions:

"The motto is 2.0 [grade average] or go! It's not higher, but it's a lot harder because you're with the best. The average that you may have gotten is an A in a regular college. That [grade] becomes a C when you're here. So it gets a lot tougher and a lot more competitive."

She also discussed some of the other requirements that demand midshipmen's time and energy:

"Once a semester you have to pass three physical tests. You have to pass the Applied Strength Test—that's where you do situps and pullups—and we have the obstacle course. You have to do the mile and one-half run and you have to do them in those standards. [The academy sets a standard for the minimum number of repetitions that must be completed in a certain time period or the maximum time in which the particular fitness activity must be completed]. Most of the standard testing you have every semester. Some semesters you might have to pass swimming, boxing, or other sports, and self-defense. Those sports are required. But most of the time, I don't think the physical standards should really phase anyone. People come in **plebe summer** and can't do situps. It's really sad. If you're really in poor physical shape and you can't get into shape before you're supposed to come, don't let it scare you because they do have this thing called 'subsquad' [a kind of conditioning group for those who can't meet the physical-fitness standards]. They'll put you on it and you'll get certain leeway to pass these tests. And if you fail them in a semester, they have another conditioning squad and you have to go to that every day. The whole logic is that they don't want to fail people. They want to pass people and that's why they have a lot of these things set up. Women get slower running times and slower obstacle course times. And, as you go up in rank, they do increase the standards. They make them more difficult.

You're required to do either intramurals or play a varsity sport. My three-and one-half years, I played a varsity sport, which I really enjoyed. I thought that helped a lot, 'cause if you're a woman on a woman's team, you have all that female bonding."

Andrea mentioned the activities that she found to be the most time-consuming:

"I don't think it's the intramurals that create a big time demand. It's all the **formations.** You have to make morning quarters, the meals, things like room formals, uniform inspection, drill in the afternoon, march-off practices, lots of little things that sort of eat up your time. It's hard to get used to it, at first when you have to be at noon meals at such and such a time and you have to do this and this. If you went to college, you could divide your schedule up how *you* want to. But, if you come here, you pretty much have to accept what courses [they offer] and how they're scheduled, and what you're going to get."

Some students are surprised by the amount of structure in the academy environment and have a hard time adjusting to the rigid demands. Andrea discussed this aspect of student life:

"It's very hard for some people to adjust [to the structure]. A lot of people didn't expect it. And the reason for structure is time management. I think people do realize that from early on. Once in awhile you'll have a plebe who doesn't understand why it's set up the way it is and that it is to teach you time-management skills—to be where you're supposed to be at the right time. If you're not there when you're supposed to be, later on when you're in the fleet, that could mean somebody's life. It could be a real serious incident. And it's professional courtesy to be on time, because that sets your reputation. That's why there is a lot of structure."

Midshipmen enter the academy with various expectations; some of these expectations are accurate and some are not. Andrea discussed how the actual experiences fit with her expectations:

"I thought all the physical things were a lot easier than I expected. I was expecting physical torture, I guess. They do look after you if you're not in top shape. The academic and the mental side was a lot more pressure than I ever imagined. You have to memorize so many things during plebe summer and there's very little time. But it really helps, because you develop rapid memorization skills. It's only for a short time, but the mental pressure is probably the toughest. It's a lot harder than the physical, I think.

For me, mental pressure is lots of memorization of things and being able to spit back something you learned maybe a long time ago. You're put on the spot. Most of the women who come in here had no idea what an M-16 [rifle] is compared to an M-60 [rifle]. They probably think they're the same thing. I think some of the guys may have had more background dealing with little guns and tanks and things girls didn't."

Teamwork and forming strong links with others is an important part of one's entire military experience. Service members at all levels, officer and enlisted, need to conform to the military standards, to all rules and procedures. The high value placed on teamwork is evident in the earliest days at the academy. Group membership and cooperation help the midshipmen adjust to the academy experience. Andrea discussed the importance of teamwork:

"Teamwork is essential. You have to be part of the team. If you're not part of the team, you're going to be left behind. [During] plebe summer, we teach people that keeping their classmates' loyalty is essential. If one of your classmates is falling behind in a platoon run, you pick him up and take him with you. You tell the guy in the front to slow down the pace. You look out for your classmates. If one of your classmates is in trouble, academically, you offer him some help. You say, 'Hey, I know this subject. Why don't you come up to my room and I'll show you how to do this problem.' I've also gone to guys and told them I'm really doing bad in this class. I had one guy spend three days tutoring me in the subject so I could pass the final exam."

The emphasis on teamwork and loyalty to one's classmates continues throughout midshipmen's years at the academy and forms the basis of strong connections that will last throughout an officer's military career. Along with this is the high value placed on honesty.

An entering midshipman during "plebe summer" at the Naval Academy.

Andrea also expressed positive feelings about this part of academy life:

"One thing I also like is the honors system. You don't have to lock anything up. If you lend something to someone, they'll bring it back. People don't just take other people's stuff, not even pencils and pens. And, if they borrow something from your room—like a book or something—and you weren't in, they leave you a message, 'I borrowed your book and I'll be in such and such a place. If you need it back, please call me.'

If someone said they did something, then you know it's done. If you give an order to someone and they say they'll do it right away, you know they'll do it right away."

Teamwork and the honors system are two specific aspects of academy life that have contributed to Andrea's positive evaluation of her experience. But there are other aspects that she has found enjoyable and valuable.

"The summers are fantastic! When you're a youngster, you get to go on a 'youngster' cruise. You get hands-on experience of knowing what it's like to lead people. You hang out with those guys and you learn what they're like. And then, you take another cruise. I went all around Florida on a little ship. You get hands-on training driving the ship [and] calling out commands.

[During] second-year classes you go around and you see all these military facilities. We have women's week and it shows you all the jobs in the military that women do. Men, that week, go down in submarines and do submarine training. Other than that, everything is the same. We do the same public speech classes, leadership [classes], and you have a few law classes. You have The Law of Armed Conflict [class], so if you were in a conflict situation [you know] what the rules are.

We're open to worldwide events. I think being in the military, being at this academy, you're more concerned about what goes on in the world. [You] pay more attention to what foreign nations are doing. As a plebe, you're required to read three newspaper articles a day, and two of them have to be on major world events. Whereas, if you went to a local college, you'd be more concerned with going into business and not with how your country looks to other nations.

Also, you become more aware of your public image. Normal college students probably [wouldn't] really care about how they look, what attitude they're presenting to other people. But here, you're really conscious about every action you do and what it means to somebody else: how it's reflected to your company officer, how it's reflected among your classmates, and how it's going to reflect back on you. You build a reputation from the day you set foot in this place and that hurts or helps you.

You grow a lot, you mature. You become more responsible, I think. You might also learn to set up good social skills, [to] develop friends, relations that might help you later on in your career. Because, when you're here, you know that you're going to be seeing everyone else and dealing with them in the fleet."

Andrea Lemon graduated from the Naval Academy in May 1991 with a bachelor's degree in engineering. After graduation, she went to job-specialty training to become a Supply Corps officer. Her service obligation is for five years. Looking into the future, she thinks that she may like to stay in the Navy until retirement. However, if she chooses to resign, sometime after she has completed her obligation, she feels confident that she will find a job in the civilian workforce.

"I'm an ocean engineer, that's my major. I could get a job working for any engineering firm. It's really applicable and more so than just the academics. People here [at the academy] know how to lead people. They know how to motivate people and get them to work and that's a big help and a big incentive."

In the remaining pages of this chapter, Katherine Elizabeth Simonson, a member of the freshman class shares a brief description of her first year at the academy.

Katherine Elizabeth Simonson

Kathy Simonson grew up in Michigan, but lived abroad before entering the Naval Academy. Her father's job with the Center for Disease Control required the family to live in Germany, and Kathy attended schools for family members of persons who worked for the United States government. Although Kathy's family does not have a history of military service, as Andrea Lemon's did, Kathy met and

Midshipman Katherine Elizabeth Simonson

made friends with military families. One family friend who was in the military influenced Kathy's decision to apply to the academy.

"There was one family in particular. I met the three daughters through various sports activities. We had different conferences through the DoD schools. And we'd also have tournaments for the different sports I was in. I met these girls through the tournaments and I'd either lose to them or beat them. So we got to know each other and got to become good friends. Their father attended the Naval Academy and graduated in 1968. He's a SEAL and he's just as good a role model as anybody."

Besides the influence of friends, Kathy discussed some of the other factors that motivated her to consider the academy:

"It's kind of obvious for a lot of people. I mean, the financial help you can get by going through here. And, I guess, reading all the catalogs they send out and talking to different people, the commanders, the friends. If you're used to putting yourself up to a lot of challenges it's kind of an attractive situation, or the thing to do. My entire life, I played sports. I played in a small city in Michigan and they didn't have a lot of only girl sports. And so I was the tomboy kind. I was always the only girl on the guys' team. And so it was fun to beat the odds and go against the norms. And I kind of see the academy as being that. It's only ten percent [female]."

Kathy's parents' reactions are especially pleasing to her.

"My parents never suggested it to me, I just did it on my own. They were always excited about it. They would have been happy if I would have gone to the University of Michigan, but I think seeing me at the academy just lightens up their eyes. I mean, I'm not doing it for them, but my entire life I've just reached for those challenges. And I guess it makes me happy to see my parents proud."

Her acceptance at the Naval Academy has been one of the major highlights in Kathy's life. She remembers her thoughts when she graduated from high school:

"I remember my mom last year. She asked me what my biggest accomplishment was in four years. I was salutatorian in my class. And I worked for that. I might have said being second in my class was most important. But it hit me, around graduation, that it was receiving my appointment to the Naval Academy. I had to do just everything. You had to be like the All-American person, just make your life this package. Receiving that appointment was like the biggest accomplishment! Because, when you look at the numbers and you look at the statistics you know how many people wanted to go and they applied and they didn't get accepted. [It's] just kind of an elite feeling."

Kathy discussed some of her feelings about her first year as a midshipman and pointed out the values the academy tries to impart:

"A lot of things that they try to ingrain in us from the beginning is that you shouldn't be here just to survive. You should be here to excel! Although your attempts might fall short, you have to strive for that. I've gotten a lot out of this year. Hard work definitely pays off. I was so scared that I would do poorly, academically, here. And that acted like a stimulant for me to get on the ball. I did pretty well this year, academically. I ended up with a 3.45, thank you."

A day at the academy is highly structured and both mentally and physically demanding. Midshipmen arise at 6:30 A.M. for a personal fitness workout and breakfast. They form for muster and inspection before attending four one-hour classes. Around noon they meet in formation to go to the meal as a group. After lunch there are two class periods followed by a two-and a-half hour period for athletics and extracurricular and personal activities. After the evening meal, which follows the activities period, all midshipmen have a study period. This ends at 11 P.M., with lights out for freshman. The study period for members of the upper classes ends at midnight.[9]

Time management is a concern for all midshipmen, especially for freshmen. Kathy was no exception. She remembers her early weeks at the academy:

"The first six weeks I was just overwhelmed! There's so much dead, free time in high school. Here there's not. It's all one big juggling act. This semester I had six classes every Monday, Wednesday, and Friday. So, the night before, if you have homework in every one of those classes, there's no way that you'll be able to do it all. So you have to prioritize. It's the biggest juggling act I've ever done."

Like Andrea Lemon, Kathy knows the importance of teamwork and support from one's peers in helping her succeed at the Naval Academy. All Naval Academy students are called midshipmen. The whole student body, about 4,000 members, is the Brigade of Midshipmen. There are six battalions in the brigade. Each battalion is made up of six companies. There are approximately 120 midshipmen in each company, which includes men and women from all four classes. This is an especially important group, since many activities and experiences are shared with members of one's own company.[10]

Kathy has very strong feelings about the role of her fellow midshipmen:

"I think the most help you get is from people in your own company, the plebes, your classmates. Since we're all taking the same classes, certain people are going to be good in one subject, whereas others can help me in others. It's all a matter of give and take and helping out all the time. I was lucky to have a really intelligent roommate. I've got two, in fact. One is just a super math student. I never had calculus before I got here and luckily, she turned me on to it. She made it easier and helped me out. I had a great teacher, luckily, too, but if I was struggling just a little bit, I would just have to ask [my roommate]. And then, if she had trouble in Chemistry I, I could help her out. It's not like you go to someone and say, 'Hey, if you help me out, I'll help you out with this.' If someone is good at something, they're willing to do it."

While the women at the Naval Academy tried to reinforce each other's confidence, Kathy has observed that some male midshipmen hold negative attitudes toward women:

"I didn't hear it, but I've got several friends who are sophomores and they heard one of their upper class say, 'I don't think women should be here. They're all out of shape and they can't meet the standards. Their standards are low.'

I think that the guys here are very smart. They don't hassle us or ride us or essentially harass us. They know they can't do that. [But] there are certain [males among the] upper class that you can just tell don't want women here. They don't come up and say, 'I don't want you here.' They can get themselves in a lot of trouble saying stuff like that. But you can still tell."

Being away from home, being responsible for one's self and adjusting to new people and a new environment, can create uncertainty. Just like students in civilian colleges, midshipmen experience stress. The structure of life at the academy is a major source of stress. And there are personal reactions as well. Kathy recalls an especially stressful time and some of the things that helped her through this period:

"A lot depends on your **squad** and that is like your family. I had a really high expectation squad and I got really stressed out. It usually happens when plebes go back for Christmas break and they get in touch with their civilian life. [They] wear civilian clothes, talk to all their friends who had their earliest class at 11 A.M., and [they get] stressed out because they had thirteen hours [of classes]. But I came back and I was gung ho. I was ready to tackle another challenge."

The situation changed as Kathy met and began to work with junior class members of her squad.

"My second class [juniors] are excellent performers. And I was kind of scared and a little intimidated. I hadn't had them in my squad before, so I didn't know them that well. They were in my classes and I was getting frustrated because I wasn't doing as well. I was getting tired and falling asleep in my classes. And I just reached a point where I hated it and I just wanted to quit. I remember, it was this one weekend, I was studying for this Naval Science exam and I just couldn't get it. I tried so hard and I had asked for help and I just had this mind block. And I called my parents and said I'm quitting. I hate this place! I just stressed out. I tried too hard, I think. I tried to make everyone else happy, except myself. I think that each midshipman has to be number one in himself. They can have faith in God, it's all your own personal choices. You've got to be happy for yourself; not to make parents happy. And so when I told them, they just couldn't believe it, because I had been so happy. I just kind of freaked out. My roommates were the greatest! They helped me sort out my life. It was just all that stress and all these little things, like getting up in the morning and delivering newspapers—doing chow calls."

The demanding and highly structured days, along with the many expectations midshipmen experience, can be a major source of stress. Kathy believes that moderation, setting goals, and the support from her roommates helped her through a stressful time.

"I wanted to have my grades high. I wanted to do good militarily. Because the first semester I got a 3.6, but I think it was useless because I didn't get an A in military performance. So that was one of my goals this semester. Like I said, it was moderation. I was lucky because I had cool roommates. It is that support that helped me. I talked to my roommates all the time and stayed up past taps (the signal for lights out) and just talked forever. My squad definitely had the family element that may have made it worth staying."

Looking back at her freshman year, Kathy has positive feelings about staying at the academy. She talked briefly about her plans after graduation and her choice of occupation:

"I want to go to medical school and I think the Navy's medical corps is probably the best out of all the services. I think being in Germany and going to all the different military hospitals helped me see a lot because I never really wanted to be a doctor for the money. I just wanted to do it because I've always been interested in it. And I just see medicine *and* the military as great. There's a lot of benefits and I think they [the military] concentrate more on the job and on doing it well."

Both Andrea Lemon and Kathy Simonson, despite some difficulties, are pleased with their choice to become midshipmen. Both look forward to exciting careers as naval officers.

The four major paths to becoming a military officer have been discussed in this chapter. In addition, there is a fifth path that is available to a small number of people. Each branch of the service has an Enlisted Commissioning Program that allows qualified enlisted members to earn officer commissions through one of the pathways discussed earlier. These programs vary somewhat from one branch of the service to another. This path is the smallest source of officers to the armed forces, supplying ten percent of the new officers who enter each year.[11]

CHAPTER
SEVEN

Looking Ahead: Future Prospects for Women in the United States Military

What does the future hold for women in the United States military? This may seem like a simple question, but there is no simple, direct answer. People have different opinions about what the future will be, but one thing we do know is that the future holds many possibilities. In Chapter 5 you were introduced to Sergeant Earnestine Richardson, an enlisted woman in the Army. She commented on the future:

"The future holds numerous opportunities for women in the military. I believe the future is exciting and positive, offering diverse career choices."

You were introduced to Captain Barbara Nyce in Chapters 1 and 2. Although Captain Nyce is retired from the Navy, she continues to be interested in the evolving role of military women. She offered her thoughts about their opportunities for the future:

"I think the future prospects for women in the military are exciting and positive *and* will be slow to change. Based on the testimony of the Chief of Naval Operations at recent congressional hearings, I don't think the most recent changes in legislation [1991 provisions passed by Congress and mentioned in Chapter 3] will result in significant improvements for Navy women right away. For some exasperating reason, discrimination against military women solely on the basis of gender seems to be acceptable at all levels of our society. Women will continue to pressure for new assignment areas to be opened to them because they are qualified. They must guard vigilently against doors being closed to them only because they are women."[1]

When asked if she thought women should be permitted to serve in combat, Captain Nyce responded with the following comments:

"The use of the word 'permit' annoys me. Who is authorized, and by whom, to do the permitting? Whether in a draft or volunteer environment, women should be assigned in exactly the same manner as men. The criteria for assignment, whether intellectual, physical, physiological, or any combination thereof, should be the same for both men and women. With the leaner military force now required, it is wasteful to allow false barriers to prevent what might be the better qualified person from filling a particular billet."

These are the thoughts of some military women, one still serving and one who is retired. What about the views of men associated with the military?

Sean O'Keefe, a civilian, who was the acting secretary of the Navy addressed the midshipmen at the Naval Academy in January 1993. He spoke in favor of removing all restrictions that prevent women from serving on combat aircraft and all naval ships, including submarines and amphibious vessels. He also believes that women should be required to register with the **Selective Service** and be subject to **conscription**, if reinstated, on the same basis as men.[2]

General Colin Powell, chairman of the Joint Chiefs of Staff, also spoke to the midshipmen in January 1993. General Powell reportedly said that the military had to open more opportunities to women but should not remove the restrictions for ground combat.

The American public also has opinions about women's military service. At present the public is supportive of women serving in some, but not all, combat jobs. The idea of women in ground combat is the most emotional issue and the one that meets the most resistance. However, public acceptance of women in some combat roles has increased in recent years. Perhaps this has something to do with society's changing attitudes about women in general. Also, the performance of military women in the Persian Gulf helped change public attitudes. As columnist Ellen Goodman stated: "The Gulf War will be remembered as the time when military myths met reality and women soldiers came into their own."[3] Americans recognized the reality of modern warfare: fighting is a high-tech operation and there is no clearly defined battlefront. Women in the Gulf War were exposed to danger, risk of injury, capture, and death even though they were not officially assigned to combat jobs.

In 1991 Congress responded to public opinion and women's performance in the Gulf War. As mentioned in Chapter 3, the House of Representatives and the Senate passed legislation that included provisions for the following: removal of the 1948 restrictions barring women from combat aircraft in the Air Force, Navy, and Marines (this implied changes in Army policy); appointment of a fifteen-member presidential commission to study the assignment of military women; and waiving of the remaining combat exclusion law so that tests could be done on the assignment of women to all combat jobs while the newly created commission examined the issues. It is important to note that the legislation *allowed*, but did not *require*, the services to assign women to combat jobs. This gave the services a great deal of freedom in the assignment of military women.[4]

The Presidential Commission and Its Recommendations

The Presidential Commission on the Assignment of Women in the Armed Forces heard the testimonies of civilian and military experts, read research reports from the Department of Defense and social scientists who study related issues, examined surveys, and went on fact-finding missions in the United States and abroad. The commission's report, handed down in November 1992, made recommendations on seventeen issues related to the assignment of military women. All of the recommendations are important for the future of military women. However, the following discussion focuses on those that are most directly related to the issues of women in combat and conscription.

In terms of the general issue of opening combat jobs to women, the commission recommended that military readiness should be the major determinant of assignment policies and that there are *some* situations in which women might be assigned to combat positions. As for more specific combat jobs for women, the commission recommended that women *not* be assigned to ground combat units or positions or to combat aircraft, but that women *could* be assigned to combatant vessels, except submarines and amphibious vessels.

The specific recommendations of the presidential commission are especially interesting in relation to the 1991 legislation that would allow women to serve on combat aircraft. The commission disagreed with the earlier decision and recommended that the 1948 restriction be reenacted. However, the vote was close: eight supported the recommendation and seven opposed it. Those in favor of reenactment of the 1948 restriction were concerned about the presence of women affecting the cohesion of male units and the possibility of women being taken as prisoners of war.

Also interesting is the commission's recommendation that women be assigned to combatant vessels. If this recommendation is followed, Congress will have to repeal the only remaining combat exclusion law from 1948. Keep in mind that the 1991 legislation did not remove it. The main reasons for keeping the exclusion for submarines and amphibious vessels is concern for privacy and living space. Both types of vessels are crowded and confined and it would be costly to modify them.

In general, the commission's view of women in ground combat units and jobs is similar to the ideas of the American public and many service members.

The issue of registering women with the Selective Service and drafting them (if the American military were to re-instate the draft) along with men is not as emotional as is the issue of women in combat. Still, it is a concern to those who are interested in the future of military women. The commission recommended that women not be required to register and not be drafted even if men are.[5] While some people will be pleased with this recommendation, others will see it as denying women equal opportunity to serve and relieving them of equal responsibility for service to the country.

Reactions to the Commission's Report

The reactions to the commission's report have been mixed. Most civilians and military personnel who oppose women's assignment to combat jobs were satisfied with the recommendations. Others, who favor offering women more opportunities, reacted negatively and criticized the commission for being too conservative. Military personnel and interested civilians wondered what effect the commission's recommendations would have on the future of military women. In general, it was believed that major changes were not likely to occur in the near future because senior military officials still had a lot of freedom in making policies related to the assignment of military women. The officials from an older generation are not likely to support rapid change.

The Barriers Begin to Fall

On April 28, 1993 the final barriers for United States military women began to fall when Defense Secretary Les Aspin announced new policies for the assignment of women. The Secretary lifted the ban on women in combat aviation jobs and directed the Navy to begin increasing sea-duty assignments for women. Mr. Aspin announced that he would ask Congress to repeal the 1948 law that prohibited the assignment of women to combat ships. He also ordered the services to review all combat jobs that remain closed to women and to justify the continued exclusion of women from these positions.

The broad changes will open more than 20,000 jobs on ships and aircraft that have previously been held only by men. These jobs are important for advancement to the highest military ranks so women's opportunities for promotion should increase.[6]

Changes By Branch

As mentioned in Chapter 3, the Air Force has selected seven women for combat training and soon more will be offered the opportunity. They will fly fighters and bombers and may be assigned to squadrons with men in early 1994.

Navy women will soon enter specialized training for F/A-18 Hornets and F-14 Tomcats (fighter jets). Female pilots who have served as instructors and test pilots and have participated in training exercises may soon be assigned to combat squadrons based on aircraft carriers. In fact, if the 1948 law is repealed, the Navy will open most combat slots to qualified women over the next few years. It is likely that they will be continued to be prohibited from serving on submarines and amphibious vessels.

Female pilots in the Army will soon be training for combat

missions in Apache and Cobra attack helicopters. Positions in other units are likely to become available after the Army studies the possibility of opening field artillery, air defense, and other combat units to women.

Currently there are no female pilots in the Marine Corps, but change is on the way. Qualified women will begin flight training and compete with males for aviation slots. The Marine Corps will also review the possibility of opening positions in units previously closed to women.[7]

At this time there are plans to reduce the size of the United States military. This process is known as "downsizing." As a result of downsizing, the services' needs, missions, and readiness levels will undergo change. Opportunities for all service members—women and men—will be in flux. Since the Department of Defense has expressed a commitment to providing women full and equal opportunity, women should not be given special consideration to stay in nor should they be targeted for discharge.

In addition to Department of Defense policies, public opinion and the attitudes of society about the "appropriate" roles for women and concerns with equal opportunity will affect the future of women in the armed forces.

So, to return to the question posed at the beginning of this chapter: What does the future hold for women in the United States military? There is no simple, direct answer; there do seem to be many exciting possibilities. Some of the possibilities are quite new so it is difficult to predict how quickly changes will occur. When thinking about the future of military women, it is important to remember that the purpose of the military is to protect and defend the interests, ideals, and commitments of the United States. While equal opportunity is a concern, the focus has to be on military effectiveness. It is hoped that future military assignment policies will match service members' qualifications with job requirements. Any such decisions will be based on an individual's capabilities and performance, not gender. It appears that the military is heading in this direction.

Whatever the future holds, the long history of women's involvement in military activities demonstrates that women are willing and able to serve their country.

★ ★

Epilogue

Have you ever thought about joining the military? After reading this book, maybe you will consider the possibility. What does serving in the military mean to you? Is it different from working in a civilian job? Is military service a "calling" that involves the sacrifice of your own self-interest for a higher purpose, that of protecting and defending national interests? Or is it like a job in the civilian society where personal concerns such as salary, fringe benefits, working conditions, and job satisfaction are most important?

There are many answers to these questions because Americans are a diverse group of people with different backgrounds and experiences that influence their individual attitudes. The military women interviewed for this book represent different experiences based on background and environment. All have a view of the relationship between themselves as citizens and their nation. And this view affects their definition of service. Over the years, ideas about this relationship have changed along with changes within society.

In the early history of the United States, service to the nation was seen as an obligation of citizenship. Service in the military was thought to be a "calling" that involved personal sacrifice. Slogans such as "duty, honor, and country" were associated with service, and those who joined were respected by others. Citizenship rights, such as the right to bear arms and the right of protection by the state, were earned by meeting the obligation. This view of citizenship emphasized responsibility more than rights.

Over the years, obligations and rights were given more equal emphasis and the military began to offer more benefits, such as educational assistance and family allowances, to those who served. While the benefits grew, they were still earned in exchange for service. In fact, over time, military service became an avenue through which racial and ethnic minorities and women, who were often discriminated against in civilian society, could achieve rights and improve their situations.

The view of the relationship between citizens and the nation changed in the mid-twentieth century. The definition of citizenship began to emphasize rights over obligations. This change was associated with the growth of welfare organizations in American society and the belief that a citizen was entitled to receive benefits as a right, separate from the idea of service. This view was based on the idea that the whole society has responsibility for those who cannot take care of themselves, simply because they exist in society. This resulted in more emphasis on individuals' rights than on national responsibilities.

In addition to broader social changes, new developments in the military influenced the definition of service. At different times, the United States military has obtained personnel through conscription, that is, by drafting eligible men. When the most recent use of conscription ended in 1973, the armed forces began to rely on volunteers to meet personnel needs. With the move to the all-volunteer force, serving in the military became more like holding a civilian job. The link between citizenship and service became less important when the military had to adopt attractive employment practices in order to compete with civilian companies for employees. This promoted the change in the definition of military service. It was seen more as a job than as a responsibility of citizenship.

The recruitment efforts of the late 1970s and early 1980s emphasized personal interests and the benefits of service, such as job security, salary, skill training, educational assistance, health care, and opportunities for travel and adventure. The conditions that made military service different from civilian jobs, such as frequent moves, separation from family, long working hours without overtime pay, and risk of physical injury and death, were rarely mentioned. "Be All That You Can Be" and "Not Just a Job, An Adventure" were popular slogans from this period.

These changes in society and in the military influenced the meaning of military service for individuals. Volunteers who entered the armed forces during the 1970s and 1980s were more likely to be motivated by personal interests and job-related benefits than by a sense of obligation to serve the country.[1]

In the 1990s, there is evidence of a return to the idea of linking citizenship to service. Recruiters mention that some young people express the desire to serve their country as one reason for their wanting to join the military. Also, President Clinton has created a National Service office and has announced a plan to begin a voluntary National Service program. At this point, the plan is general and would require a person to commit a specified period of time to service to the local or national community. While joining the military would be one choice, other types of service might include working with the underprivileged in inner cities or rural areas, staffing hospitals or day care centers, or joining service organizations such as Volunteers in Service to America (VISTA) or the Peace Corps. In return for service, volunteers would receive financial assistance for a college education.

The important point in thinking about developing a national service program is returning to a definition of citizenship that includes meeting national responsibilities as well as receiving benefits. Formation of some type of national service program would tell members of society that service to the nation is necessary and valuable.

Perhaps this discussion will encourage you to think about the meaning of citizenship. What does it mean to you to be a citizen of your country? As a citizen, do you have responsibilities as well as rights? How will you respond to the words of President John F. Kennedy, "Ask not what your country can do for you, ask what you can do for your country"? And finally, if you do not think you have a national responsibility, consider this question: "If not you, who?"

Time Line

1775–1783	American Revolution
1812	War of 1812
1861–1865	Civil War
1898	Spanish-American War
1901	Army Nursing Corps is established as an auxiliary unit. Women wear uniforms for the first time.
1908	Navy Nursing Corps is established as an auxiliary unit.
1914	World War I breaks out in Europe.
1917–1918	The period of U.S. involvement in World War I Women reservists are granted full military rank and status.
1939	World War II breaks out in Europe.
1941–1945	The period of U.S. involvement in World War II
1942	Women's Auxiliary Army Corps (WAAC), Women Accepted for Volunteer Emergency Service (WAVES), and Marine and Coast Guard reserve units for women are established.
1943	Women's Army Corps (WAC) is established. WAAC is dissolved.
1948	Women's Armed Services Integration Act establishes regular, permanent military status for women and combat exclusions for women in the Air Force, Navy, and Marines.
1950–1953	Korean conflict Many, but not all, African-American soldiers serve in integrated units.
1951	Defense Advisory Committee on Women in the Services (DACOWITS) is established to assist with the recruitment of women. The DACOWITS continues to function in 1993, advising the Department of Defense on various issues related to women's military service.
1954	All-black units are abolished. African Americans are officially integrated into the armed forces.
1960s	The civil rights movement and the women's movement set the stage for many changes for women in American society and the military.
1965–1973	Vietnam conflict
1967	Congress passes legislation that removes some of the restrictions on military women's career opportunities that had been specified in the Women's Armed Services Integration Act.

117

1969	Air Force ROTC is opened to women.
1970s	The civil rights movement and the women's movement continue to improve the status of women in civilian society. Armed services offer more opportunities and open many positions to women.
1972	Army and Navy ROTC are opened to women. The Equal Rights Amendment (ERA) is passed by Congress but does not become law.
1973	An all-volunteer force (AVF) is established when the draft is ended.
1975	The first women are admitted to the United States Coast Guard Academy.
1976	The first women are admitted to the United States Air Force Academy, the United States Naval Academy, and the United States Military Academy.
1978	Women are integrated into all services with men when the separate women's branches are dissolved.
1980s	Many new opportunities and positions in the military are made available to women.
1980	Defense Officer Personnel Management Act (DOPMA) puts women on the same promotion lists as men.
1989	The U.S. invasion of Panama draws attention to women's exposure to risk and dangerous conditions even though they are officially barred from combat.
1990–1991	Persian Gulf War Women participate in large numbers and in many positions. The nature of their participation and their exposure to risk renewed the controversy over combat exclusions.
1991	National Defense Authorization Act for Fiscal Years 1992 and 1993 removes exclusions for women in combat aircraft and establishes the Presidential Commission on the Assignment of Women in the Armed Forces.
1992	Presidential commission's report is given to the president. The recommendations include continuing to exclude women from ground and air combat and allowing women to serve on combatant vessels in the Navy.
1993	The Secretary of Defense announces the lifting of the ban on women in combat aviation, effective immediately, and a plan to ask Congress to repeal the only remaining combat exclusion law (from 1948), which restricts women from serving on combat ships. The Secretary of Defense also orders all services to review and justify the exclusion of women from all other combat jobs.

Glossary

Active duty   Full-time military service.

Aircrew member   Person who performs duties supporting aircraft operations.

Air Force   The branch of the U.S. armed forces that is mainly responsible for military operations in the air.

All-volunteer force (AVF)   A military force consisting entirely of volunteers.

Amphibious vessels   Naval vessels that carry troops to land-based military operations.

Army   The branch of the U.S. armed forces that is mainly responsible for military operations on land.

Basic training   Training for new recruits that includes the basic knowledge, physical conditioning, and skills necessary for becoming a member of the military. Also called boot camp.

Billet   A specific job assignment in the Navy.

Cadets   Students at United States Air Force Academy, United States Military Academy, United States Coast Guard Academy, and in ROTC.

Canvassing   Recruiting volunteers for the armed forces.

Coast Guard   The branch of the U.S. armed forces that is responsible for protecting America's coastlines and inland waterways. It is under the authority of the Department of Transportation during peacetime. In national emergencies, it is under the authority of the Navy.

Combat exclusions   Laws and policies that keep certain people, women, for example, out of jobs and units that are involved in fighting with the enemy or that expose service members to risk of injury, capture, or death. The exclusions may be legally specified in laws or contained in policies determined by the separate branches of the service.

Commissioned Officers   Those who have been certified as officers after successfully completing one of the commissioning paths. Commissioning assigns the officer rank, authority, and obligation.

Conscription   Compulsory enrollment for military service; also called the draft.

Defense Advisory Committee on Women in the Services (DACOWITS)   A committee of civilians appointed by the president to advise the secretary of defense on issues related to the service of military women.

Defense Officer Personnel Management Act (DOPMA)   A 1980 act that resulted in the abolition of separate female promotion lists in the Army, Navy, and Marines. Women were put on the same promotion lists with men. The Air Force promotion lists had been integrated for some time.

Deferment   A temporary postponement of military service.

119

Department of Defense (DoD)   A federal agency in charge of the U.S. military.

Deployment   The movement of troops away from their home base.

Direct appointment   A path for becoming a commissioned officer that is available to certain professionals, such as doctors, nurses, lawyers, and clergy.

Draft   Also known as conscription; a method of bringing people into the military on a compulsory basis. In the history of the United States, only men have been drafted. The draft was done away with in 1973.

Duty station   A place where a service member is assigned to work for a specified period of time.

Enlistees   Persons who are in the enlisted, rather than the officer, ranks of the military.

Exemption   A basis for release from military service required of others.

Formations   Particular arrangements of military troops, such as columns or rows, for the purpose of inspection or completion of a group activity such as marching.

Fraternization   The development of close personal relationships with others.

GED   General Educational Development is a testing program developed by the American Council of Education. People who do not have a high school diploma may earn an equivalency diploma or certificate by passing the GED test battery.

Induction   Process through which one becomes a member of the military.

In-process   The process a service member goes through when arriving at a new duty station.

Marine Corps   The branch of the U.S. armed forces that is trained for missions on both land and sea. The corps is trained to respond quickly to U.S. military needs all over the world.

Midshipmen   Students at the United States Naval Academy.

MOS school   A school that offers job (Military Occupational Specialty) training for service members.

National Defense Authorization Act for Fiscal Years 1992 and 1993   Legislation signed in 1991 that included provisions to repeal combat exclusion laws (from 1948) for women in combat aircraft and established the Presidential Commission on the Assignment of Women in the Armed Forces.

National Guard   Reserve components (Air Force and Army) that support the operations of the active-duty military. They are under state authority during peacetime. In times of national emergency, such as the Persian Gulf War, they are under federal control and may be activated to assist in the emergency.

Navy   The branch of the U.S. armed forces that is primarily responsible for military missions at sea.

Noncommissioned officers (NCOs)   Enlisted persons whose rank and pay grade are between E-4 and E-9 and who frequently supervise enlistees of lower ranks.

North Atlantic Treaty Organization (NATO)   An organization consisting of the U.S. and its western European allies that was formed in 1949 to provide for the collective defense of member nations.

Officer Candidate School (OCS)   A path for college graduates without military training to become commissioned officers in the Army, Navy, or Marines.

Officer Training School (OTS)   A path for college graduates without military training to become commissioned officers in the Air Force.

Pay grades   Levels corresponding to ranks in the military. There are nine enlisted and ten officer pay grades. Salary and other allowances increase with rank and pay grade.

Pentagon   Headquarters for the Department of Defense located in Arlington, Virginia. The names Pentagon and Department of Defense are sometimes used interchangably.

Plebe summer   A seven-week indoctrination period for plebes (freshmen students) that begins on Induction Day in July and ends when the upperclassmen return for the fall semester.

Port security   Jobs that involve protecting and defending military interests in seaports.

Protocol   Jobs that involve dealing with customs and regulations associated with military formality and etiquette.

Reconnaissance   A mission that involves the gathering of information for military purposes, such as surveying the enemy's strength or position.

Recruit   A new member of the military.

Reserve Officers' Training Corps (ROTC)   A path to becoming a commissioned officer for students who are attending college. Military courses and training are combined with college courses.

Reserves   Forces that support the mission of the active-duty military. Reservists usually serve on a part-time basis but may be called to active duty in times of emergency.

Risk Rule   A rule developed by the Department of Defense in 1988 to provide uniform standards for the assignment of women across the services.

Selective Service   A federal agency that registers men so that they will be available if the military needs to return to conscription.

Service academies   Federal institutions that offer a four-year program leading to a bachelor's degree and provide a path for becoming a commissioned officer.

Service obligation   The specified period of time a person agrees to serve when joining the military. It is a legal commitment.

Services   The separate branches of the armed forces—the Air Force, Army, Navy, Marines, and Coast Guard.

Sexual discrimination   Unequal treatment of a person on the basis of his or her sex.

Sexual harassment   Unwanted and unwelcome comments or advances of a sexual nature.

Special operations   Specialty areas (requiring specific skills) in each branch of the armed services such as Navy SEALS, Army Rangers, and Green Berets.

Squad   The smallest military unit.

Stereotypes   Rigid beliefs about the way a group of people are, or should be.

Tour of duty   A period of duty at one location; also known as a "tour."

USAFA   The United States Air Force Academy in Colorado Springs, Colorado. The military academy that supplies commissioned officers to the Air Force.

USCGA   The United States Coast Guard Academy in New London, Connecticut. The military academy that supplies commissioned officers to the Coast Guard.

USMA   The United States Military Academy in West Point, New York. The military academy that supplies commissioned officers to the Army.

USNA   The United States Naval Academy in Annapolis, Maryland. The military academy that supplies commissioned officers to the Navy and Marines.

Veterans Administration   An agency that coordinates all hospitals and other agencies that provide by law benefits such as health care, educational assistance, insurance, pensions, and mortgages to military veterans.

War College   An educational institution that provides advanced training to officers. A master's degree may be earned in selected fields of study. Each of the services has a War College; there is also a National War College.

Women Accepted for Volunteer Emergency Service (WAVES)   The women's reserve unit established by the Navy in 1942. It was abolished in 1972 and Navy women were integrated into the branches with men.

Women's Airforce Service Pilots (WASPs)   Civilian women who flew all types of military aircraft overseas and served as test pilots and instructors for male military pilots during World War II.

Women's Armed Services Integration Act   Passed in 1948, this act offered women regular military status with restrictions on their service, including combat exclusions for women in the Air Force, Navy, and Marines.

Women's Army Corps (WAC)   The women's corps established by the Army in 1943 when the WAAC was dissolved. The women had regular military status. The WAC was abolished in 1978 when women were integrated into the branches with men.

Women's Auxiliary Army Corps (WAAC)   The first women's corps established by the Army in 1942. The women had auxiliary status. The WAAC was abolished in 1943 when the WAC was formed.

Yeoman (F)   Enlisted women who served in the naval reserves in World War I. They were often called "yeomanettes."

Notes

Introduction

1. Dick Cheney, *Annual Report to the President and the Congress* (Washington, D.C.: U.S. Government Printing Office, 1992), 135.

2. Research Division, *Semi-Annual Race/Ethnic/Gender Profile of the Department of Defense Active Forces, Reserve Forces, and the United States Coast Guard* (Patrick Air Force Base, Fla.: Defense Equal Opportunity Management Institute, September 1992), 12–22.

3. This summary draws heavily on the description of the similarities and differences between gender and racial integration in David R. Segal's *Recruiting for Uncle Sam* (Lawrence, Kansas: University Press of Kansas, 1989), 113–114.

4. This summary draws heavily on the thorough discussion of arguments for and against women's combat participation in Mady Wechsler Segal, "The Argument for Female Combatants," in Nancy Loring Goldman, ed., *Female Soldiers—Combatants or Noncombatants?* (Westport, Conn.: Greenwood Press, 1982), 267–290.

5. ————, "News Briefs," *Minerva's Bulletin Board* (Summer 1992), 5–11; Mark Thompson, "Tailhook report singles out 140," *Baltimore Sun* (April 24, 1993), 1A, 6A.

6. Mady Wechsler Segal, and Katherine H.M. Knudson, *Scientific Knowledge Applied to Decisions Regarding Women in the Military* (A Report to the Secretary General of NATO) (Washington, D.C.: U.S. Government Printing Office, 1985), 25–32.

7. Judith Hicks Stiehm, *Arms and the Enlisted Woman* (Philadelphia: Temple University Press, 1989), 128–129.

8. Segal, "The Argument for Female Combatants."

9. ————, *DoD Task Force Report on Women in the Military* (Washington, D.C.: Department of Defense, January 1988). Details on these issues are discussed throughout the report.

Chapter 1. Breaking Ground: Women's Early Involvement in Military Activities

1. Mary Ann Attebury, "Women and Their Wartime Roles," *Minerva: Quarterly Report on Women and the Military* (Spring 1990), 11–28; M.C. Devilbiss, *Women and Military Service: A History, Analysis, and Overview of the Key Issues* (Maxwell Air Force Base, Alabama: Air University Press, 1990), 1–2.

2. Patrick J. Leonard, Review of *America's First Woman Warrior: The Courage of Deborah Samson* in *Minerva: Quarterly Report on Women and the Military* (Fall/Winter 1992), 101–103.

3. Devilbiss, *Women and Military Service*, 2; C. Kay Larson, "Bonnie Yank and Ginny Reb Revisited," *Minerva: Quarterly Report on Women and the Military* (Summer 1992), 35–61.

4. Devilbiss, *Women and Military Service*, 2.

5. Ibid., 2–3.

6. Martin Binkin, and Shirley J. Bach, *Women and the Military* (Washington, D.C.: The Brookings Institution, 1977), 5; Devilbiss, *Women and Military Service*, 3–5.

7. Devilbiss, *Women and Military Service*, 3–5.

8. Binkin and Bach, *Women and the Military*, 7–10.

9. Ibid.; Alice A. Booher, "A Special Salute to Women Military POWs," *Minerva's Bulletin Board* (Summer 1992), 1–4.

10. Kay Gott Chaffey, video review, "Women of Courage: Story of the WASP—Women Airforce Service Pilots, World War II." *Minerva: Quarterly Report on Women and the Military* (Fall/Winter 1992), 103–106.

11. Binkin and Bach, *Women and the Military*, 6–12.

12. David R. Segal, *Recruiting for Uncle Sam* (Lawrence, Kansas: University Press of Kansas, 1989), 119.

13. Jeanne Holm, *Women in the Military: An Unfinished Revolution*, rev. ed. (Novato, Calif: Presidio Press, 1992).

14. Attebury, "Women and Their Wartime Roles," 16–17. A complete discussion of the roles of American women in Vietnam is given in Holm, *Women in the Military*, 205–242.

15. Binkin and Bach, *Women and the Military*, 13–19.

Chapter 2. Gaining Ground: The Expansion Years— 1970s and 1980s

1. Martin Binkin and Shirley J. Bach, *Women and the Military* (Washington, D.C.: The Brookings Institution, 1977), 13–17; M.C. Devilbiss, *Women and Military Service: A History, Analysis, and Overview of Key Issues* (Maxwell Air Force Base, Alabama: Air University Press, 1990), 12, 19–24.

2. M.C. Devilbiss, *Women and Military Service*, 19–24; John Gaieski, "DoD Task Force Report on Women in the Military: Update of Recommendations Under Combat Exclusions," presented to the Defense Advisory Committee on Women in the Services (Norfolk, Virginia, October 1989), 4, 15. Women who were assigned to ships in the combat logistics force (CLF) were on ships that traveled with the battle group to provide the combatant ships with support services such as supplies and refueling. The CLF ships may be close to a combat area, but do not actually take part in fighting.

3. Captain Nyce explained officer communities in the following way: "Naval officers are categorized into one of two groups: line officers and staff corps officers. *Line officers* perform jobs which are directly related to the Navy's mission. Examples of the line officer communities are the surface community, the submarine community, the aviation community, and the generalist community. Generalists are those officers who are qualified to perform a broad range of line officer jobs which do not require specific warfare expertise. *Staff corps officers* perform support functions such as health care, legal services, supply, etc. Perhaps a familiar example would better serve to distinguish between the line communities and the staff corps communities. A football team has players, coaches, trainers, equipment handlers, etc. The players and the coaches might be compared to the line [officers], and the others might be compared to the support personnel."

4. This information is no longer accurate. According to Captain Barbara Nyce, "In the aftermath of the Tailhook mess, the Navy has four line women officers on active duty who have been promoted to, or selected for, the rank of rear admiral."

5. Gaieski, "DoD Task Force Report on Women in the Military," 2–16.

6. Becraft, Carolyn, *Women in the Military 1980–1990* (Washington, D.C.; Women's Research and Education Institute, June 1990), 4, 6.

7. Charles Moskos, "Army Women," *The Atlantic Monthly* (August 1990), 71–78.

Chapter 3. Women's Current Service in the Military

1. Research Division, *Semi Annual Profile of the Department of Defense Active Forces, Reserve Forces, and the United States Coast Guard* (Patrick Air Force Base, Fla.: Defense Equal Opportunity Management Institute, September 1992), 12, 19.

2. Richard H. P. Sia, "Aspin Clears Way for Women to Fly in Combat, Prepares More Changes," *Baltimore Sun* (April 29, 1993), 3A.

3. Research Division, *Semi-Annual Profile*, 13, 20; Carolyn Becraft, *Women in the Military 1980–1990* (Washington, D.C.: Women's Research and Education Institute, June 1990), 6.

4. D'Ann Campbell, "Combating the Gender Gulf," *Minerva: Quarterly Report on Women and the Military* (Fall/Winter 1992), 13–33; *Presidential Commission on the Assignment of Women in the Armed Forces Report to the President* (Washington, D.C.: U.S. Government Printing Office, 1992), 28–29.

5. John Lancaster, "Nearly All Combat Jobs To Be Open To Women," *Washington Post* (April 29, 1993), A1, A8.

6. Committee on Women in the NATO Forces, *Women in the NATO Forces* (Brussels, Belgium: ATO Information Services, 1986).

7. Research Division, *Semi-Annual Profile*, 15, 24; Becraft, *Women in the Military 1980–1990*, 5.

8. Eric Schmitt, "Women Ready to Fly for Navy, or Flee It," *New York Times* (April 23, 1993), A14.

9. *Presidential Commission on the Assignment of Women*, 31–33.

10. Research Division, *Semi-Annual Profile*, 16, 25; Becraft, *Women in the Military 1980–1990*, 5.

11. *Baltimore Sun* (August 12, 1992), 11A.

12. Research Division, *Semi-Annual Profile*, 17, 26; Becraft, *Women in the Military 1980–1990*, 6.

13. ————, *Women in the Military: More Jobs Can Be Opened Under Current Statutes* (Washington, D.C.: General Accounting Office, September 1988).

14. Campbell, "Combating The Gender Gulf," 25–26.

15. Ibid., 24–25; Becraft, Testimony given before House Armed Services Committee (February 19, 1991).

16. *Presidential Commission on the Assignment of Women*, D–1–2.

17. Ibid., C–21–31.

18. Reuven Gal, *A Portrait of the Israeli Soldier* (Westport, Conn: Greenwood Press, 1986), 46–57.

Chapter 4. Choices for Service: Branches, Active Duty, Reserves, and National Guard

1. John Lancaster, "Nearly All Combat Jobs to Be Open to Women," *Washington Post* (April 29, 1993), A1, A8.

2. *Military Careers: A Guide to Military Occupations and Selected Military Career Paths 1992–1994* (Washington, D.C.: Department of Defense, 1992), 40.

3. Ibid., 32.

4. Ibid., 36, 44.

5. Ibid., 48.

6. Ibid., 222, 230, 238.

7. Ibid., 230, 238; *Profile Magazine* (January 1993), 8.

8. *Military Careers*, 27–30, 223–226.

9. *Army Times* (November 9, 1992), 6.

10. *Military Careers*, 30, 226.

Chapter 5. Options for Service: Enlisted and Officer Ranks

1. *Military Careers: A Guide to Military Occupations and Selected Military Career Paths 1992–1994* (Washington, D.C.: Department of Defense 1992) is the main reference source for this chapter. Some of the information has been paraphrased and some has been expanded and used in a more general way.

2. *Profile Magazine* (January 1993), 21.

3. Holly Hechter, and Elaine El-Khawes, *Joining Forces: The Military's Impact on College Enrollments* (Washington, D.C.: American Council of Education, October 1988), 19.

4. Telephone conversation with Army recruiter, Baltimore, Maryland, March 17, 1993.

5. *Profile Magazine*, 10, 23, 32, 45.

Chapter 6. Becoming an Officer: How You Get There

1. "Basic Facts About Army ROTC" (Pamphlet published by U.S. Army, December 1988); *Military Careers: A Guide to Military Occupations and Selected Military Career Paths 1992–1994* (Washington, D.C.: Department of Defense, 1992), 214; *Profile Magazine* (January 1993), 11–12.

2. *Military Careers*, 214; *Profile Magazine*, 10–11, 23, 32, 44–45.

3. *Military Careers*, 214; *Profile Magazine*, 7.

4. *Military Careers*, 213.

5. These figures are given in information sheets, pamphlets, and catalogs from the service academies.

6. The information on admission requirements and nominations is summarized from material in the current catalogs from each of the service academies. These catalogs may be obtained by writing to the addresses listed on page 130.

7. *United States Naval Academy Catalog 1991–1992*, 8.

8. The academy catalogs are the sources of the general summary of benefits and programs at the academies.

9. *United States Naval Academy Catalog 1991–1992*, 36.

10. Ibid., 33.

11. *Military Careers*, 214.

Chapter 7. Looking Ahead: Future Prospects for Women in the United States Military

1. This statement was made prior to the Navy's investigation of the Tailhook incident and the Navy's announcement of its intent to liberalize assignment policies for women

2. Joanna Daemmrich, "Navy Secretary Supports Combat Role for Women," *Baltimore Sun* (January 7, 1993), 1B, 4B.

3. Ellen Goodman, "Gulf War Shows Women Can Handle Combat," *Bloomington Times Herald Record* (April 23, 1991), 35.

4. Holm, Jeanne, *Women in the Military: An Unfinished Revolution*, rev. ed. (Novato, CA: Presidio Press, 1992), 503–505.

5. This material is taken from the *Presidential Commission on the Assignment of Women in the Armed Forces Report to the President* (Washington, D.C.: U.S. Government Printing Office, 1993). Information from several pages in the report has been summarized and paraphrased. If you are interested in reading more about the seventeen issues and recommendations, you may order a copy of the report from the U.S. Government Printing Office in Washington, D.C.

6. Richard H.P. Sia, "Aspin Clears Way for Women to Fly in Combat, Prepares More Changes," *Baltimore Sun* (April 29, 1993), 3A.

7. Ibid; John Lancaster, "Nearly All Combat Jobs to Be Open to Women," *Washington Post*, (April 29, 1993), A1, A8; Eric Schmitt, "Pentagon Plans to Allow Combat Flights By Women; Seeks to Drop Warship Ban," *New York Times* (April 28, 1993), A1.

Epilogue

1. This discussion of the link between citizenship rights and responsibilities and the changing meanings of military service draws heavily on David R. Segal, *Recruiting for Uncle Sam* (Lawrence, Kansas: University of Kansas Press, 1989). Information from several pages in the source has been paraphrased and summarized.

Further Reading

Books

Barkalow, Carol. *In the Men's House: An Inside Account of Life in the Army by One of West Point's First Female Graduates*. New York: Poseidon, 1990.

Bradley, Jeff. *A Young Person's Guide to Military Service*. Boston: Harvard Common Press, 1987.

Cornum, Rhonda, and Peter Copeland. *She Went to War*. Novato, CA: Presidio Press, 1992.

Goldman, Nancy, ed. *Female Soldiers—Combatants or Noncombatants?* Westport, CT: Greenwood Press, 1982.

Hall, Richard. *Patriots in Disguise: Women Warriors of the Civil War*. New York: Paragon House, 1993.

Holm, Major General Jeanne. *Women in the Military: An Unfinished Revolution*. Novato, CA: Presidio Press, 1982.

Hovis, Bobbi. *Station Hospital Saigon: A Navy Nurse in Vietnam, 1963–1964*. Annapolis, MD: Naval Institute Press, 1991.

Keil, Sally Von Wagenen. *Those Wonderful Women and Their Flying Machines: The Unknown Heroines of World War II*. New York: Four Directions Press, 1990.

Macdonald, Sharon, Pat Holden, and Shirley Ardener, eds. *Images of Women in Peace and War: Cross-Cultural and Historical Perspectives*. Madison: The University of Wisconsin Press, 1987.

Military Careers: A Guide to Military Occupations and Selected Military Career Paths, 1992–1994. Published by the U.S. Department of Defense, Washington, D.C., and available from the U.S. Government Printing Office, Washington, D.C.

Schneider, Dorothy, and Carl J. *Sound Off!: American Military Women Speak Out*. New York: E.P. Dutton, 1988.

Stiehm, Judith Hicks. *Arms and the Enlisted Women*. Philadelphia: Temple University Press, 1989.

Wekesser, Carol, and Matthew Polesetsky, eds. *Women in the Military*. San Diego, CA: Greenhaven Press, Inc., 1991.

Journals/Magazines

Armed Forces and Society
Department 4010
Transaction Periodicals Consortium
Rutgers University
New Brunswick, New Jersey 08903

An international, interdisciplinary journal that is published quarterly. It includes articles on a variety of topics related to the study of the military.

Minerva: Quarterly Report on Women in the Military
The Minerva Center
20 Granada Road
Pasadena, Maryland 21122-2708

This easy-to-read volume is devoted to topics related to women in the military. Also included are book reviews and recent publications relevant to the subject.

Profile Magazine
DoD High School News Service
Profile Magazine
1877 Dillingham Blvd.
Norfolk, Virginia 23511-3097

This magazine provides young people and guidance counselors with information about various aspects of military service. It is published monthly November through April.

Addresses for the United States Military Academies

Air Force

Admissions Office
HQ USAFA/RRS
United States Air Force Academy
Colorado Springs, Colorado
80840-5651

Army

Director of Admissions
United States Military Academy
606 Thayer Road
West Point, New York
10996-9902

Coast Guard

Director of Admissions
United States Coast Guard Academy
15 Mohegan Avenue
New London, Connecticut
06320-4195

Navy and Marines

Candidate Guidance Office
United States Naval Academy
Annapolis, Maryland
21402-5018

Table 1 — General Enlistment Qualifications*

Age	Must be between 17 and 35 years. Consent of parent or legal guardian required if 17.
Citizenship Status	Must be either (1) U.S. citizen, or (2) an immigrant alien legally admitted to the U.S. for permanent residence and possessing immigration and naturalization documents.
Physical Condition	Must meet minimum physical standards listed below to enlist. Some military occupations have additional physical standards.

Height — For males: Maximum - 6'8"
                     Minimum - 5'0"

Height — For females: Maximum - 6'8"
                       Minimum - 4'11"

Weight — There are minimum and maximum weights, According to age and height, for males and females.

Vision — There are minimum vision standards.

Overall health — Must be in good health and pass medical exam. Certain diseases or conditions may exclude persons from enlistment; for example, diabetes, severe allergies, epilepsy, alcoholism, and drug addiction.

Education	High School graduation is desired by all services and is a requirement under most enlisted options.
Aptitude	Must make the minimum entry score on the Armed Services Vocational Aptitude Battery (ASVAB). Minimum entry scores vary by service and occupation.
Moral Character	Must meet standards designed to screen out persons likely to become disciplinary problems. Standards cover court convictions, juvenile delinquency, arrests, and drug use.
Marital Status and Dependents	May be either single or married; however, single persons with one or more minor dependents are not eligible for enlistment into military service.
Waivers	On a case-by-case basis, exceptions (waivers) are granted by individual services for some of the above qualification requirements.

---

*Each service sets its own enlistment qualification requirements. If you are interested in a specific service's enlistment requirements contact a military recruiter.

Source: Military Careers

Table 2 — Pay Grades and Ranks for Enlisted Members

SERVICE / PAY GRADE	ARMY	NAVY	AIR FORCE	MARINE CORPS	COAST GUARD
E-9	COMMAND SERGEANT MAJOR / SERGEANT MAJOR	MASTER CHIEF PETTY OFFICER	CHIEF MASTER SERGEANT	SERGEANT MAJOR / MASTER GUNNERY SERGEANT	MASTER CHIEF PETTY OFFICER
E-8	FIRST SERGEANT / MASTER SERGEANT	SENIOR CHIEF PETTY OFFICER	SENIOR MASTER SERGEANT	FIRST SERGEANT / MASTER SERGEANT	SENIOR CHIEF PETTY OFFICER
E-7	SERGEANT FIRST CLASS	CHIEF PETTY OFFICER	MASTER SERGEANT	GUNNERY SERGEANT	CHIEF PETTY OFFICER
E-6	STAFF SERGEANT	PETTY OFFICER FIRST CLASS	TECHNICAL SERGEANT	STAFF SERGEANT	PETTY OFFICER FIRST CLASS
E-5	SERGEANT	PETTY OFFICER SECOND CLASS	STAFF SERGEANT	SERGEANT	PETTY OFFICER SECOND CLASS
E-4	CORPORAL SPECIALIST	PETTY OFFICER THIRD CLASS	SERGEANT SENIOR AIRMAN	CORPORAL	PETTY OFFICER THIRD CLASS
E-3	PRIVATE FIRST CLASS	SEAMAN	AIRMAN FIRST CLASS	LANCE CORPORAL	FIREMAN SEAMAN
E-2	PRIVATE	SEAMAN APPRENTICE	AIRMAN	PRIVATE FIRST CLASS	FIREMAN APPRENTICE SEAMAN APPRENTICE
E-1	No Insignia PRIVATE	SEAMAN RECRUIT	No Insignia AIRMAN BASIC	No Insignia PRIVATE	No Insignia SEAMAN RECRUIT

Source: Military Careers

Table 3 — Summary of Enlisted Employment Benefits

Vacation	Leave time of 30 days per year.
Medical, Dental, and Eye Care	Full medical, hospitalization, dental, and eye care services for enlistees and most health care costs for family members.
Continuing Education	Voluntary educational programs for undergraduate and degrees or for single courses, including tuition assistance for programs at colleges and universities.
Recreational Programs	Programs include athletics, entertainment, and hobbies:

Softball, basketball, football, swimming, tennis, golf, weight training, and other sports

Parties, dances, and entertainment

Club facilities, snack bars, game rooms, movie theaters, and lounges

Active hobby and craft clubs, book and music libraries.

Exchange and Commissary Privileges	Food, goods, and services are available at military stores, generally at lower cost than regular retail stores.
Legal Assistance	Many free legal services are available to assist with personal matters.

Source: Military Careers

Table 4 — General Officer Qualifications*

Age

Must be between 19 and 29 years for OCS/OTS; 17 and 21 years for ROTC; 17 and 22 years for the service academies.

Citizenship Status

Must be U.S. citizen.

Must meet minimum physical standards listed below. Some occupations have additional physical standards.

Physical Condition

Height — For males: Maximum - 6'8"
                       Minimum - 4'10"

Height — For females: Maximum - 6'8"
                       Minimum - 4'10"

Weight — There are minimum and maximum weights, According to age and height, for males and females.

Vision — There are minimum vision standards.

Overall health — Must be in good health and pass medical exam. Certain diseases or conditions may exclude persons from enlistment; for example, diabetes, severe allergies, epilepsy, alcoholism, and drug addiction.

Education

Must have a four-year college degree from an accredited institution. Some occupations require advanced degrees or four-year degrees in a particular field.

Aptitude

Must achieve the minimum entry score on an officer qualification test. Each service uses its own officer qualification test.

Moral Character

Must meet standards designed to screen out persons unlikely to become successful officers. Standards cover court convictions, juvenile delinquency, arrests, and drug use.

Marital Status and Dependents

May be either single or married for ROTC, OCS/OTS, and direct appointment pathways. Must be single to enter and graduate from service academies. Single persons with one or more minor dependents are not eligible for officer commissioning.

Waivers

On a case-by-case basis, exceptions (waivers) are granted by individual services for some of the above qualification requirements.

---

*Each service sets its own enlistment qualification requirements. If you are interested in a specific service's enlistment requirements contact a military recruiter.

Source: Military Careers

Table 5 — Pay Grades and Ranks for Officers

PAY GRADE / SERVICE	ARMY	NAVY	AIR FORCE	MARINE CORPS	COAST GUARD
O-10	GENERAL	ADMIRAL	GENERAL	GENERAL	ADMIRAL
O-9	LIEUTENANT GENERAL	VICE ADMIRAL	LIEUTENANT GENERAL	LIEUTENANT GENERAL	VICE ADMIRAL
O-8	MAJOR GENERAL	REAR ADMIRAL (UPPER HALF)	MAJOR GENERAL	MAJOR GENERAL	REAR ADMIRAL (UPPER HALF)
O-7	BRIGADIER GENERAL	REAR ADMIRAL (LOWER HALF)	BRIGADIER GENERAL	BRIGADIER GENERAL	REAR ADMIRAL (LOWER HALF)
O-6	COLONEL	CAPTAIN	COLONEL	COLONEL	CAPTAIN
O-5	LIEUTENANT COLONEL	COMMANDER	LIEUTENANT COLONEL	LIEUTENANT COLONEL	COMMANDER
O-4	MAJOR	LIEUTENANT COMMANDER	MAJOR	MAJOR	LIEUTENANT COMMANDER
O-3	CAPTAIN	LIEUTENANT	CAPTAIN	CAPTAIN	LIEUTENANT
O-2	FIRST LIEUTENANT	LIEUTENANT JUNIOR GRADE	FIRST LIEUTENANT	FIRST LIEUTENANT	LIEUTENANT JUNIOR GRADE
O-1	SECOND LIEUTENANT	ENSIGN	SECOND LIEUTENANT	SECOND LIEUTENANT	ENSIGN

Source: Military Careers

Table 6 — Summary of Employment Benefits for Officers

Vacation	Leave time of 30 days per year.
Medical, Dental, and Eye Care	Full medical, hospitalization, dental, and eye care services for officers and most health care costs for family members.
Continuing Education	Voluntary educational programs for undergraduate and graduate degrees or for single courses, including tuition assistance for programs at colleges and universities.
Recreational Programs	Programs include athletics, entertainment, and hobbies:

Softball, basketball, football, swimming, tennis, golf, weight training, and other sports

Parties, dances, and entertainment

Club facilities, snack bars, game rooms, movie theaters, and lounges

Active hobby and craft clubs, book and music libraries.

Exchange and Commissary Privileges	Food, goods, and services are available at military stores, generally at lower cost than regular retail stores.
Legal Assistance	Many free legal services are available to assist with personal matters.

Source: Military Careers

136

INDEX

active duty, 1–2, 34, 49, 85
  requirements of, 57
Air Force, 1, 21, 33, 34, 54–56,
  77–84
  job assignments in, 28, 36–37,
  55
  in Persian Gulf War, 43
  Reserve, 57
  training for, 67, 111
  see also National Guard
Air Force Academy (USAFA), U.S.,
  28, 87, 91
  admission to, 88–89
all-volunteer force (AVF), 28
American Revolution, 9–11
amphibious vessels, 37, 110
Anderson, Richard, *see* Clark,
  Amy
Army, 1, 14, 16, 21, 26, 33, 34,
  69–72
  Air Corps, 54
  job assignments in, 28, 30, 37, 55
  Rangers, 73
  Reserve, 57
  training for, 67, 111–12
  see also National Guard
Arnold, Dorothy, 18
Aspin, Les, 34–35, 36, 37, 55, 111
Assistant Chief of Naval Person-
  nel for Women, 25

Barkalow, Carol, 48
Barton, Clara, 12–14
basic training, 23, 70
  length of, 67
  for officers, 74–75, 79
  for women vs. men, 39–40
benefits, for military personnel,
  14, 17, 29, 68, 69
  educational, 58, 59, 60, 62, 64,
  89–90, 114
  medical, 64, 89, 114
  retirement, 26, 58, 60, 64
Black, Malinda, 11
Boyd, Belle, 11
Bradley, Ruby, 18
branches:
  combat training in, 111–12
  job assignments in, 34–38
  overview of, 54–56
  women's, 16–18
  see also specific branches
Brantley, Hattie, 18
Bray, Linda, 33
Bush, George, 36

career development, 7, 32, 42
casualties, 44, 51

Chezek, Mike, 38–40
children, 71
  care of, 7, 49, 60–61
civilian labor force, 19–21
civil rights movement, 27
Civil War, 11–13
Clark, Amy, 12
Clinton, Bill, 115
Coast Guard, 1, 16, 17, 34, 56
  job assignments in, 38, 56
  in Persian Gulf War, 43
  Reserve, 57
Coast Guard Academy, U.S.
  (USCGA), 28, 87–89
  admission to, 88–89
Cochran, Jacqueline, 18
Cold War, 21–22, 75–76
combat, women in, 9–12, 18,
  108–11
combat exclusion laws, 21, 29, 32,
  33, 34, 35, 36, 38, 40, 69–70,
  71, 73, 109, 110
commissioned officers, 55, 86, 91
Congress, U.S., 27, 35, 37, 63, 76,
  89, 107, 109, 110, 111
conscription, 108, 109, 114

Defense, U.S. Department of
  (DoD), 1, 5, 7, 22, 28, 29, 32, 34,
  40, 49, 109, 112
Defense Advisory Committee on
  Women in the Services
  (DACOWITS), 22
Defense Equal Opportunity Man-
  agement Institute, 70
Defense Officer Personnel Man-
  agement Act (DOPMA) (1980),
  31
Deputy to the Assistant Chief of
  Naval Personnel, 31
direct appointment, 73, 87
Dix, Dorothea Lynde, 12
draft, 18, 26, 27, 56, 108, 110, 114
duty station, 68, 75–76

education:
  advanced training, 75
  assistance in, 58, 59, 60, 62, 64,
  69, 89–90, 114
  continuing, 75
  of enlisted personnel, 67–69, 70
  of officers, 73–76, 85–106
  professional, 75, 91
Eisenhower, Dwight D., 22
Elliott, Marie, 44–48
Enlisted Commissioning Program, 106
enlisted personnel, enlistees, 55,

65–72, 89
  job specialties for, 66
  qualifications for, 66
  training and eduation of, 67–69
equal opportunity, 29–30, 40, 112
Equal Rights Amendment (ERA),
  27

family policy, 49
Flynn, Jeanne, 36
Foote, Pat, 51
foreign militaries, 52–53
fraternization, 6

Goodman, Ellen, 109
Green, Mary Jane, 11
Green Berets, 73
Greet, Lila, 11
Grenada, 33

health care, *see* medical benefits
Hobby, Oveta Culp, 16
homosexuality, 6–7

induction, 67
integration, 21, 26, 30–31, 52
Israeli Defense Force (IDF), 53

job assignments, 7, 18, 24, 28, 30,
  32, 51–52, 60, 66, 70, 72–73,
  88, 111
  by branch, 34–38
job-specialty training, 68, 100
  for enlisted personnel, 66
  for officers, 72–73, 75, 80, 88
joint-service couples, 49, 60, 70

Kennedy, John F., 23, 115
Korean conflict, 2, 22, 49

Lemon, Andrea Louise, 91–100,
  106
lesbianism, 6–7
Libya, 33
London, Barbara Jean Erikson, 19

McAfee, Mildred, 16
Marine Corps, 1, 16, 17, 21, 34,
  55–56
  job assignments in, 30, 37–38,
  56
  in Persian Gulf War, 43
  Reserve, 14, 15, 57
  training for, 40, 67–68, 112
Mayfield, Grace Binge, 19
medical benefits, 7, 32, 46, 64, 69,
  114
men, military:
  women compared with, 3–5

women resisted by, 2, 6, 36, 93
midshipmen, 91–106
Military Academy, U.S. (USMA), 28, 48, 87
  admission to, 88–89
Military Careers: A Guide to Military Occupations and Selected Career Paths, 1992–1994, 65
Military Occupational Specialty (MOS) school, 40
"Molly Pitcher," 9

National Defense Authorization Act for Fiscal Years 1992 and 1993, 36
National Guard, 34, 44–48, 58–62, 72, 85
National Service Office, 115
Naval Academy, U.S. (USNA), 28, 87, 91–106
  admission to, 88–90, 93
Navy, 1, 6, 16, 17, 21, 24–25, 26, 34, 56
  job assignments in, 30, 35, 37, 55
  in Persian Gulf War, 42–43
  Reserve, 14, 15, 57
  training for, 67, 111
Nelson, Mary Rose Harrington, 18
Nestor, Helen Cassini, 18
nominations, to service academies, 89, 93
noncommissioned officers (NCOs), 55
North Atlantic Treaty Organization (NATO), 22, 52, 53
nurses, 9, 12–14, 22, 26
Nursing Corps, 14, 15
Nyce, Barbara Regina, 23–25, 30–32, 107–8

Officer Candidate School/Officer Training School (OCS/OTS), 73, 74, 79, 80, 86–87
officers, 72–84
  job specialties for, 72–73, 88
  qualifications for, 73
  responsibilities of, 72
  training and education of, 73–76, 85–106
O'Keefe, Sean, 108

Panama, 33
pay, 25, 29, 63–64
  for enlisted personnel, 69
  for officers, 76
Peace Corps, 115
Pentagon, 36, 81
Persian Gulf War, 1, 34, 42–52, 58, 60–61, 82, 108–9
  Air Force in, 43
  casualties in, 44, 51
  Coast Guard in, 43
  job assignments in, 42

Marine Corps in, 43
  as "Mom's War," 49
  National Guard in, 44–48
  Navy in, 42–43
  wounded in, 44
  prisoners of war in, 44, 51
Powell, Colin, 108
Presidential Commission on the Assignment of Women in the Armed Forces, 109–11
  reactions to, 110–11
prisoners of war, 12, 18, 44, 51, 110
promotion, 31–32, 35, 83, 111

rank, 14, 15, 40–42, 69, 76
  see also promotion
recreational facilities, 7, 32
recruitment, 7, 14, 24, 28, 37, 38–39, 66, 72, 77, 86, 114, 115
  standards used in, 38
recruits, 68
Recruit Training Command for Women, 24

Reserve Officers' Training Corps (ROTC), 28, 73, 74–75
  admission to, 85
  cadets, 74, 85
  curriculum of, 85–86
  service obligation of, 86
reserve units, 1–2, 17–18, 34, 57–58, 72, 85
  see also specific reserve units
retirement, 26, 58, 60, 64, 71
Richardson, Earnestine, 69–72, 107
"Rosie the Riveter," 19
Rossi, Marie, 51

salary, *see* pay
Samson, Deborah, 10–11
Schwarzkopf, H. Norman, 48–49
SEALS, 73
Secretary of Defense, *see* Aspin, Les
Secretary to the Chairman of the Joint Chiefs of Staff, 31
selective service, 108, 110
service academies, 73, 74, 87–91
  admission to, 87–88, 89–90
  curriculum of, 90–91
  honor system of, 97–98
  nominations to, 89, 93
  resignations from, 94–95
  stressful nature of, 104–6
  summer activities of, 99
  teamwork emphasized at, 97, 103–4
service obligation, 56, 86, 91
services, *see* Air Force; Army; Navy; Marines
sexual discrimination, 5, 7, 61–62,

80–81, 107–8
sexual harassment, 5–6, 32, 81
Seymour, Dawn Rochow, 19
Shurtliff, Robert, *see* Samson, Deborah
Simonson, Katherine Elizabeth, 100–106
Spanish-American War, 13–14
special operations, 72–73
Strevig, Deborah, 58–62

Tailhook incident, 6
tour of duty, 68
Townsend, Kathryn Lindsay, 77–84, 86
training, *see* basic training; education; job-specialty training
Transportation, U.S. Department of, 1, 34, 38, 56
Tubman, Harriet, 11

United Nations, 53

Veterans Administration (VA), 19, 64
Volunteers in Service of America (VISTA), 115

Walker, Mary E., 12
War College, 31
West Point, *see* Military Academy, U.S.
Whittle, Reba Zitella, 18
women, military:
  African-American men compared with, 2–3
  attitudes toward, 48, 71, 80–81, 82, 93, 94, 104, 108–9, 112
  clout of, 24, 30–32
  men compared with, 3–5
  discharges of, 10, 11, 12, 29, 39
  early involvement of, 9–26
  future prospects for, 107–15
  male resistance to, 2, 6, 36, 93
  Middle Eastern culture and, 47
  stereotypes of, 4–5
Women Accepted for Volunteer Emergency Service (WAVES), 16
Women Airforce Service Pilots (WASPs), 18–19
Women's Armed Services Integration Act (1948), 21, 26
Women's Army Corps (WAC), 17–18, 28–29
Women's Auxiliary Army Corps (WAAC), 16–17
women's movement, 27
World War I, 14–15, 26
World War II, 16–19, 21, 26, 51

yeomen (F), defined, 14